THE END IS IN SIGHT

Bible-based resources for youth groups

Ten sessions on Revelation for 13-18 year olds

Written by Steve Tilley and Ian Kitchen

CONTENTS

THE END IS IN SIGHT

CONTENTS

How to Use This Book	Page 3
Useful Books	Page 5
Revelation: What's the Fascination?	Page 6
Revelation and Apocalyptic Literature	Page 7
Characters in the Book of Revelation	Page 9
Quiz	Page 10
Using Revelation to Help your Group Praise and Pray	Page 11
Need to Focus on Jesus	Page 12
Session 1 VISION ON (Revelation 1)	Page 13
Session 2 THE GOOD, THE BAD AND THE STRUGGLING (Revelation 2 & 3)	Page 18
Session 3 WHO GOES THERE? (Revelation 4 & 5)	Page 23
Session 4 SHELTER FROM THE STORM (Revelation 6:1 - 8:5)	Page 28
Session 5 ENVIRONMENTAL HEALTH (Revelation 8:6 - 11:18)	Page 33
Session 6 FILTH SANDWICH (Revelation 11:19 - 14:13)	Page 38
Session 7 TIME, EVERYONE, PLEASE (Revelation 14:14 - 16:21)	Page 43
Session 8 WHO'S MIGHTY NOW? (Revelation 17:1 - 19:10)	Page 48
Session 9 WINNERS AND LOSERS (Revelation 19:11 - 22:5)	Page 53
Session 10 ENDING UP! (Revelation 22:6-21)	Page 58
About CYFA/Pathfinders	Page 63
Other resources from CPAS	Page 64

How to Use This Book

Reading

The book of Revelation is exciting stuff. It needs to be read in a lively way. We're great fans of Eugene Peterson's *The Message* (Navpress) to convey the emotion of a passage, although it is a paraphrase not a translation. *The Dramatised Bible* (Marshall Pickering/Bible Society) also has some interesting ways of tackling bits of Revelation. Look at it.

Each session is based on a long chunk of the text but will have one or two key portions. It is a good idea to be in the habit of reading the whole passage when you meet. This will enable your group to get the drift of the sequence of the whole thing and will prevent them thinking, as we may sometimes suggest, that the Bible can only be tackled in ten-verse chunks.

Why not start the Revelation programme with an evening set aside for reading the whole book? Use candle-light, background music and have a couple of breaks for refreshments. It will probably take you a couple of hours.

About us

Actually we lied. This is about you. There is no short cut to teaching Revelation to your group. You need to know the book yourself pretty well first. *The End is in Sight* will help you stay one jump ahead. So we haven't made it the sort of tool that you can just take into your meetings and do without preparation. You thought we had? Tush. Sorry!

So make yourself comfortable (not too comfortable, Denis), and read Revelation through. Now speed read *The End is in Sight*. Get the feel.

Some sort of plan

Please don't plan to cover the subjects in this book in ten consecutive sessions. It's a bit heavy. Do three or four weeks on Revelation and then take a break and try something lighter. Many of the other CYFA publications include sessions that can be done as 'one-offs'. Alternatively, have an evening devoted to worship, prayer or just having social time together.

Please make sure you plan, in general terms, a few weeks in advance. This will enable you to get together any equipment, or the occasional hard-to-track-down video clip or piece of music.

Please select and adapt. Each session contains too much material and is written by people who do not know the personal circumstances of your group. Make sure that what you plan meets your needs.

The sessions

Each session of *The End is in Sight* is divided into:

- ◆ Teaching Point
- ◆ Group Aim
- ✎ Equipment Checklist
- ☞ Leaders' Guide
- ☞ Bible Background
- ➤ Starting It, Teaching It and Doing It – The main teaching content.
- ✎ Work-out – copyright-free, photocopiable pages for members.

HOW TO USE THIS BOOK

Non-secret code — We have used the following code to help you select from the activities listed under Starting It, Teaching It and Doing It:

✪ ✪ ✪ **Essential** This section covers the key thoughts of the passage and provides enough material for about thirty minutes' teaching.

✪ ✪ **Desirable** Good supplementary stuff to take the session up to about an hour. Includes some lighter material.

✪ **Additional** Extra material for groups of different abilities, ages, sizes and tastes. Includes other light-hearted things.

Pray — Yeah! Do it. Please.

Relationships — Most of the members of your group will remember you and forget everything you ever said. That is to say, if you lead a consistent life, with your teaching and your lifestyle making sense of each other, they will learn from your example as well as your teaching. So they will apply the teaching to their lives and, probably, forget who taught it them. This is good.

If your teaching and your lifestyle are inconsistent you will spoil the teaching message. Nobody will pay any attention to it because you don't, apparently, pay any attention to it yourself.

The end of the line is that relationships with your members are important. If you only meet once a week they will take ages to get to know you and learn how to learn from you.

Penny-pinching — You can be. This book is designed so that the group only needs one copy and you can photocopy the Work-out sheets for your group. If – of course – you are privileged enough to have multiple leaders and you want to buy a copy for each leader we are not going to stop you and it will hasten the day of CPAS's global market domination.

The next book — CYFA staff love producing these resources and value feedback. Tell us how easy it is to use. Tell us if it's disappointing, and, if possible, why. Let us know if there are Bible books or themes you would like to see tackled in future books. Talk to us.

Useful Books

We have found many useful books in preparing this material. We'd like to point you towards the following titles as being particularly helpful:

New Testament Introduction (Revised Edition), Donald Guthrie, Apollos, 1990

New Testament Foundations Vol.2: Acts – Revelation,
Ralph P. Martin, Paternoster, 1978

Revelation (New Century Bible Commentary),
G. R. Beasley-Murray, Marshall, Morgan and Scott, 1975

Revelation (Tyndale New Testament Commentaries), Leon Morris, IVP, 1984

The Message – The New Testament in Contemporary Language,
Eugene H. Peterson, Navpress, 1993

Reversed Thunder – The Revelation of John and the Praying Imagination,
Eugene H. Peterson, Harper, San Francisco, 1988

Revelation Unwrapped – Revealing the Blessing of John's Vision,
John Richardson, MPA Books, 1996

The Future of Humanity – Revelation 4 to 22,
Murray Robertson, The Bible Reading Fellowship, 1993

End of Story – What Jesus Said About the Future of the World,
Stephen Travis, IVP, 1997

Christ Will Come Again, Stephen Travis, Hodder and Stoughton, 1997

The Church Under Fire, Stephen Travis, Bible Reading Fellowship, 1995

The Message of Revelation (The Bible Speaks Today),
Michael Wilcock, IVP, 1975

Revelation: What's the Fascination?

Young Christians get dead excited about the book of Revelation. If they belong to a Bible study group they will probably have suggested studying it. Even those whose contact with the Christian community is merely tentative will be aware of the book's power to fascinate.

What has caused this? Here are three possible reasons:

People used to be attracted by the past, assembling family trees, telling stories of family history and being proud of their culture. The onset of technology turned attention to the future. Why think about the past when the future is so rosy? More technological advance has taken place since the Second World War than took place in all the years leading up to it. People became optimistic and ceased looking back.

Then came nuclear threat (1960s and 70s), famine (1980s) and global warming (1990s). Suddenly the future wasn't so bright that we had to wear shades. People immersed themselves in the present – now-ism, to coin a phrase. By and large, people are not aware of their roots and only live for the moment. Consequently anything that throws light on what the future will be like has an allure: astrology, forecasts, predictions and a whole load of movies about alien invasion are the result. In the light of this, Revelation's vivid and powerful portrayal of the end of all things attracts many new students.

But secondly, the images of Revelation continue to have a powerful hold. Even those who have not studied the book carefully will appreciate some of its dark themes. Anyone who has had more than a brief conversation with a Jehovah's Witness will be aware of the value they place on Revelation, often swallowing the symbolism at the expense of the truth it symbolizes.

Thirdly is the whole mystery element. Revelation sits there at the end of the Bible, giving clear information about God's judgement and wonderful encouragement to Christians under persecution, and yet is rarely studied. Would it be rude to suggest that many young people, thumbing through their Bibles during a dull sermon, will have found themselves captivated by the language of Revelation and wondering what it means?

There may be more reasons. Whatever, it is our experience that if you ask a youth fellowship what they would like to study, the book of Revelation is regularly in the top three. (The other two are sex/relationships and the Genesis creation accounts.) Yet for years there has been no response from the Church, assuming that the study would be too hard.

We contend that a careful study of Revelation *is* hard, but is not too hard. If your young people are fascinated, that's your greatest single ally.

Revelation and Apocalyptic Literature

Revelation is part of the school of Apocalyptic literature. As a type it is common in the Bible and was widespread between 200 BC and AD 100. It is uncommon today. Perhaps some of the work of American novelist Frank Peretti *(This Present Darkness; Piercing the Darkness)* falls into this category and maybe some science fiction writing, but little else. What are the characteristics of apocalyptic literature?

- It sees life as part of God's purpose, leading to a conclusion by God's intervention.

- It makes heavy use of picture language and symbolism, especially the symbolism of number and colour.

- It offers hope and promise to people suffering persecution.

The other examples in the Bible are in **Isaiah 24-27, 56-66, Zechariah 9-14, Joel, Ezekiel's** visions and **Daniel 7-12**.

Revelation displays these characteristics, but also some distinctives too.

- It is delivered by a contemporary figure, John, who is known to his readers and is a fellow sufferer. This is in contrast to the apocalypses in the Bible's apocryphal books (1 Enoch, 2 Baruch, 4 Ezra) which were attributed to a famous person from the past.

- It is not exclusively apocalyptic. It is set in the form of a letter, yet describes itself also as prophecy.

- It speaks directly to the sufferer's current situation. It is the light of the future shining on the present. (So we will find it impossible to understand today unless we get to know the situation of Revelation's original readers/hearers.)

'This season he's been a real revelation,' said the football manager on *Match of the Day*. He was describing the improvement in the performance of a young full-back. What did he mean? Well something like, 'He's revealed something of himself that we didn't know about before – new depths of skill, or perhaps stamina.'

So, for someone to be 'a revelation', they need to reveal something new about themselves.

The noun 'revelation' has its root in a Latin word *revelare*. Since *velare* means 'to veil', *revelare* means the opposite, 'back to veil', or 'to unveil'. The book

REVELATION AND APOCALYPTIC LITERATURE

'Revelation' is therefore an unveiling. As we read it we must expect things to be revealed that were previously hidden. What things?

Well the first three verses of chapter one give us a clue:

It is revelation from God, of Jesus, through an angel, to John, written down and read, eventually by us. We can expect to be blessed if we read it and take it to heart. Whereas a game of Chinese whispers will result in a message being distorted as it passes from person to person, those involved in the transmission of this message are reliable; they are either heavenly beings (God, Jesus, an angel) or those entrusted with the message (John and perhaps his scribe). We can be sure that what God wanted to be revealed about Jesus Christ in this book has been faithfully preserved. Information about Jesus has been revealed, but it is not new. Where was it hidden?

Interestingly enough, it was hidden elsewhere in Scripture. Revelation is not the unveiling of new information; it is the making clear of old information. It was always there.

This gives us our first clue about understanding Revelation, the book. We need to look carefully at that which Scripture says clearly in other places as we study what Revelation says in pictures. Want to know about Jesus' return? Read **I Thessalonians 4&5**. Want to know about Jesus, the Lamb of God? Read one of the Gospels. Want to understand the new creation in **Revelation 21&22**? Read about the original creation in **Genesis 1-3**.

So let's embark on our journey through the Revelation to St John the Divine, remembering to expect it to reveal things rather than obscure them. If at any point you feel the text is making things difficult, remember to look for what else the Bible has to say on the subject. It will always help.

Characters in the Book of Revelation

Most of these characters are dealt with in more detail in the teaching sessions, but here's an overview of the main people, animals and other beings who catch the eye during the course of John's vision. Numbers in brackets refer to the chapters where they crop up.

Someone 'like a son of man' (1, 14) – that's Jesus, using a title from Daniel's great vision in the Old Testament book of, er, Daniel.

One on the throne (4, 20) – God himself; specifically, the Father.

Twenty-four elders (4, 19) – beings, probably angelic, with a priestly function of offering worship to God.

Four living creatures (4, 19) – representing the entire range of living things in creation.

The Lamb who had been slain (5, 14, 19) – Jesus, who was sacrificed in the place of God's people.

Four horsemen (6) – among the more memorable of the many agents God uses to carry out his judgement on the earth.

One hundred and forty-four thousand people – or the 'great multitude' (7, 14, 19) – a symbolic number, standing for all the countless numbers of people God will save through Jesus.

Two witnesses (11) – the context and symbolism remind us of Moses and Elijah, who were expected to precede the coming of the Messiah, and also of the priest and king about whom the Old Testament prophet Zechariah speaks. They represent the Church's costly but ultimately triumphant witness to the world about Jesus.

The first woman (12) – the community of God's people.

The dragon (12, 20) – Satan.

The child (12) – Jesus, destined 'to rule the nations'.

Michael (12) – traditionally, the chief angelic defender of God's people.

The beast from the sea (13) – godless political systems.

The beast from the earth (13) – godless, false but enticing and apparently powerful religion.

CHARACTERS IN THE BOOK OF REVELATION

The false prophet (16, 19) – another symbol of deceptive pseudo-religion.

The second woman (17) – 'Babylon', who lures people away from God by a promise of splendour, wealth and luxury.

The beast she sits on (17) – a massively powerful empire, set against God and his people.

The bride (19) – God's people, finally united with their Lord, Jesus.

The rider on the white horse (19) – Jesus himself, in victorious mode.

Eric (19) – the white horse. Only joking.

This doesn't explain, of course, what part all these play as the story unfolds, alongside other assorted angels, martyrs and so on. You'll need to work through the rest of *The End is in Sight* to find out that!

And here's the quiz! How well do you think you know the story? Try this quiz at the beginning, the middle or the end of your look at Revelation and see how you – and your group – get on. Just fill in the whole word wherever there's a capital letter. We'll start with an easy one.

1. R is the 27th B in the N T
2. 666 is the N of the B
3. 7 L to the C in the P of A
4. 24 E on the T
5. 4 A at the 4 C of the E
6. S in H for ½ an H
7. 7 B of G W
8. S B for 1000 Y
9. 4 L C covered with E
10. 3 E S that looked like F

(Answers, should you need them, are below. If they don't make sense, you may find you have the page the wrong way up.)

---

1. Revelation is the 27th book in the New Testament
2. see Revelation 13:18
3. 7 letters to the churches in …
4. see Revelation 1:4
5. see Revelation 4:4
6. see Revelation 7:1
7. see Revelation 8:1
8. see Revelation 15:7
9. see Revelation 20:2
10. see Revelation 4:6
10. see Revelation 16:13

PAGE 10

Using Revelation to Help your Group Praise and Pray

We're inclined to think that it's hard to spend time in Revelation without automatically finding yourself praising and praying. Still, it may help to have a bit of structure to work from. There are lots of ideas in the teaching sessions, but here are some more which may kick-start things for your group.

Praise   Revelation is very visual, because apocalyptic writing is almost like writing a cartoon strip. So use loads of visual activities in praise. Make things; use craft stuff; pick up the visual images and try to reproduce them.

If you have room outside, make a chain of beacons for lighting one by one, to reflect the sequence of events unfolding in different sections of the book – the seven trumpets and so on. Inside you could achieve something similar but less spectacular with candles. Whichever, please remember safety and don't sue us.

Revelation contains a number of songs of praise (see especially, but not exclusively, chapters 4, 5, 7, 11, 12, 15, 16, and 19). So sing. Or chant. Or praise God to a rhythm. Or whatever suits your group's culture, in musical terms. You could set the words of the book to rhythms, or work from those original words to produce something that rhymes and can be set to an existing tune, or find existing songs or hymns which use words from Revelation (there are more than you might think). Or just get the group to write their own praise songs. It's exciting!

Prayer   Use the idea of 'unveiling' (the literal meaning of 'apocalypse') as a starter for prayer. Have information or topics on a board and uncover them one by one for people to pray about. Blindfold people and take them to a beautiful place, then take the blindfold off and let them express what they feel about that revelation of God's creation. Construct something along the lines of an Advent calendar, for opening bit by bit or in a single session as you work through Revelation. Place prayer topics and starter activities under the flaps.

Revelation is a very 'corporate' book, in the sense that it gives a clear picture of salvation as something that is given to the people of God, rather than to individuals acting on their own. So build up a habit of praying for the wider church – your local church, churches in your area, the church nationally, Christians around the world, and so forth.

Please pray for us as well, and for the work we do for the church on a national (and wider) level. Thank you.

Need to Focus on Jesus

He is the image of the invisible God, the firstborn over all creation. For by him all things were created: things in heaven and on earth, visible and invisible, whether thrones or powers or rulers or authorities; all things were created by him and for him. He is before all things, and in him all things hold together. And he is the head of the body, the church; he is the beginning and the firstborn from among the dead, so that in everything he might have the supremacy. For God was pleased to have all his fulness dwell in him, and through him to reconcile to himself all things, whether things on earth or things in heaven, by making peace through his blood, shed on the cross. **Colossians 1:15-20**

We cannot see the Father. But when we focus on Jesus we see an image of the Father. Furthermore, the job of the Holy Spirit is to draw attention to Father and Son (**John 16:13-16**). Trinitarian youthwork is therefore, paradoxically, Jesus-centred.

Throughout your study of Revelation there will be temptations to be over-interested in the dark side.

Revelation stars Jesus. It's his revelation (**Revelation 1:1**). He appears as Son of man (**1:13**), slain Lamb (**5:6**), child (**12:5**) and rider on white horse (**19:11**). The book ends with his promise to come again (**22:20**) and the sharing of his grace with its readers (**22:21**).

We suggest that you use worship times to focus on the person and work of Christ and use prayer times to give thanks, regularly, for all that Christ achieved on our behalf on the cross.

Any spiritual work that involves teaching about the darker side of creation, death and judgement ought, of necessity, to focus on Christ as powerfully and regularly as possible. After all, Christians are party to good news. Let's not keep quiet about it.

SESSION 1: REVELATION 1

Vision On

◆ TEACHING POINT
The book of Revelation does have something to say to us today.

◆ GROUP AIM
That the group should understand the nature of the book and be prepared to allow it to speak to them.

EQUIPMENT CHECKLIST

(Depending on which sections you tackle, you may need)
- Copies of the Work-out sheet or prepared sheets of your own
- Bibles
- Pens
- Paper
- A copy of the Greek alphabet
- Prepared visual aid

LEADERS' GUIDE

The ten sessions we have produced require you to get to grips with Revelation yourself before you have any chance of helping your group to understand it. So, please, do some background reading before you start this session.

Always allow questions, but be prepared to side-step any that will be answered later (another reason to get an overview first). How about starting a 'Question Chart'? Write up your group's questions about Revelation as they ask them. Tick them off when dealt with. At the end of session 10 you can revisit any unanswered questions or have a summing up 'session 11'. Clever, eh?

BIBLE BACKGROUND

Material in chapter 1 tells us a lot about the whole book. It therefore acts as an introduction to the study of Revelation as well as a study of the chapter itself.

Revelation or Apocalypse (**1:1**)? Apocalypse is a Greek word. The book was written in Greek. *Apokalupsis* is the first word of the book and is translated 'revelation' in most Bibles. Hence the title.

John *who* (**1:1**)? Good question. The only well-known New Testament writer called John was John the apostle and author of the fourth Gospel, but the style here is different. Not that that is conclusive; good authors can write in more than one style and Revelation was written while the author was 'in the Spirit' (**1:10**). This John counts himself as a fellow-sufferer (**1:9**). The jury is still out (and probably isn't coming back) on John's exact identity and whether the same John wrote a Gospel, three letters and Revelation. It needn't bother us over much.

Is this prophecy? Yes; it claims to be (**1:3**), but it's also a letter (**1:4**) and the

SESSION 1

written result of a spiritual vision (**1:10-11**). Anyone who has ever tried to write down a dream will know the difficulties John faced.

Where did it come from? From God, to Jesus Christ, to an angel, to John (**1:1**), to the seven churches of Asia Minor (**1:4**), to us, his servants (**1:1**).

What's the big picture? It's Jesus-centred (**1:1-2,5-7,9-20**). It's about heaven and the end of time, 'what must soon take place' (**1:1**).

When will all this happen? Soon (**1:1**). But that word might also be translated 'suddenly'. The apocalyptic material in Daniel concerns what would happen in 'the last days'. John's revelation has a subtle twist. The start of the Christian community sees the start of 'the last days'. This gives Revelation instant impact. What heaven will be like in the future is of urgent importance now.

Is the book Trinitarian? Yes, for sure. John's greeting to the churches (**1:4-5**) is in the name of God, the Holy Spirit and Jesus Christ. God the Father is described here as the one 'who is, and who was and who is to come'. The Spirit is described as sevenfold, or 'seven spirits'. Is that because of the perfect nature of the one Spirit? Is it the Spirit whose gifts are sevenfold? Is it the Spirit equally available to each of the seven churches? Perhaps it arises from the sevenfold description of the Spirit in **Isaiah 11:2**. Scholarly opinion is divided. Michael Wilcock writes: 'we are duly warned that for some of the locked doors of Revelation, keys may be hard to find' (*The Message of Revelation*, IVP). Jesus is the central character of Revelation.

Visions – aren't they unreliable? Depends. If you or I see visions then we might put it down to spirituality, or a deadly combination of tiredness and that fruity little Cabernet Sauvignon we had last night. God's servant John was a suffering Christian, in the Spirit, on the Lord's Day. The Revelation vision, although hard to follow in some places, clearly accords with other scriptures and is consistent with what we know of Christ. **Verses 9-20** offer a picture of Jesus, risen from the dead and prepared to reveal mysteries.

➤ STARTING IT

Beginning with beginners
⭐ ⭐

Use your local knowledge to research your group's favourite books, films, songs and TV programmes. Then find out the first line of text, dialogue or lyric (or TV theme-song lyric) appropriate to each one. List them on a sheet and ask the group to match the correct opening to the correct work. We've put some on the Work-out sheet. They may help. The answers are:

1E   2A   3B   4F   5D   6C

Make the point that we learn a lot about things from their beginnings and that we learn very important stuff about the purpose of Revelation from its opening verses. Read the first three-and-a-half verses.

SESSION 1

Pictures of heaven
✪ ✪ ✪

We all have our own pictures of heaven. Give your group pencils and a copy of the Work-out sheet. Ask them to write about heaven, or draw a picture of it. Then display the pictures. In future sessions on Revelation, ask members to spend a few moments looking at their original picture and considering if they wish to alter it in the light of the passage they have studied.

Alpha and Omega
✪

The Lord God describes himself thus (**1:8**). Later (**1:17**) Jesus calls himself 'the First and the Last'. Show your group, if you can, a copy of the Greek alphabet and get them to learn to draw the symbols for these, the first and last letters. The upper case is shown first, then lower:

A or α   Ω or ω

You may want to point out that the lower-case letters look like a fish and a bum – before someone else does.

➤ TEACHING IT

John who?
✪ ✪ ✪

Read **1:9-11**. Use a flipchart to show this:

John
S
S
S
S
StW
S

Go through **1:9-11**, completing the visual aid with the following words and offering a brief explanation at each point.

John, the author of Revelation was...

Suffering, as were the people to whom he was writing. They were enduring persecution. He was in prison on the island of Patmos. On the Lord's Day, which, since the resurrection of Jesus, meant...

Sunday. He describes himself as, 'In the...

Spirit – but we need not be over-concerned about the precise 'how and why' of that sentence. He could have been worshipping deeply; he might have dreamed or become entranced. Whatever, he made himself receptive to the voice of God, as must we. He couldn't have been completely 'out of it', for he was told to do something practical – to get something to write on, a...

Scroll, and as the vision played before his very eyes he had to...

See, then **W**rite. John's words are a description, as accurate as he could make it, of what he saw. When written down, he was required to...

PAGE 15

SESSION 1

Send the completed work to the seven churches. The details of the specific message to each church are in chapters 2 and 3, but as God's servants we know that the message of the whole vision is for us too.

Jesus in disguise ✪

To make the point that John was disturbed in his worship by the voice 'like a trumpet', choose a volunteer to sit with their back to the rest of the group. Get one person to come and speak from behind them and see if the voice can be identified. Do this as a game if you want, but the point doesn't need more than one playing to make. John turned round to identify the voice.

We often fall into the trap of thinking that our Christian lives would be easier if only Jesus spoke clearly to us. It's not that simple. John didn't recognize the voice (he had to turn round) and he didn't immediately recognize the speaker, One 'like a Son of man'. Christian experience always requires interpretation in the light of what we know from Scripture.

Saw, heard, did ✪ ✪

Get members to talk about an experience from the past week. Ask them to focus on three things: what they saw, heard and did. Make the link with John's vision (**1:12-20**). He saw things, heard things and did things.

Explain that John saw:

- *Seven golden lampstands* (representing the seven churches)
- *One 'like a Son of man'* (an expression from **Daniel 7:13** and Jesus' self-depiction in Mark's Gospel)
- *Dress sense* (the speaker was dressed splendidly and flamboyantly)
- *Seven stars* (explained in **1:20** as the angels of the seven churches)
- *Sword-tongue* (a sword is an image of the word of God and its cutting power; look at **Ephesians 6:17**)

Explain what John heard:

- A voice like a *trumpet* (**1:10**) then *rushing waters* (**1:15**)
- A *claim* to be the risen one (**1:18**)
- A *second claim* to hold the keys to death (**1:18**)
- A *command* to write (**1:19**)

Explain what John did:

- *Turned round* (**1:12**)
- *Looked* and *saw* (**1:12**)
- *Fell* at his feet (**1:17**)
- *Felt* a touch (**1:17**)

▶ DOING IT

'At Your Feet We Fall' ✪ ✪

The song of this title (in most modern hymn books) is based on **Revelation 1:12-18**. Go through the words line by line, drawing out the connections. Then, if your group is into singing as worship, sing it. If not, perhaps you can get hold of a tape with it on and simply listen to it in silence.

Memory verse ✪ ✪ ✪

Revelation 1:8
'I am the Alpha and the Omega,' says the Lord God, 'who is, and who was, and who is to come, the Almighty.'

WORK-OUT

BEGINNING WITH BEGINNINGS

Here are five quotations. Down below, but not in order, are their sources. Match them up.

Quotations

1. Well, no one told me it was meant to be this way.
2. It was a bright cold day in April, and the clocks were striking thirteen.
3. In the beginning was the Word, and the Word was with God, and the Word was God.
4. 1 to 1 Courier Services
5. The mole had been working very hard all the morning, spring-cleaning his little home.
6. All this talk of getting old; it's getting me down.

Sources

A. *1984* by George Orwell
B. *John's Gospel,* New International Version
C. *The Drugs Don't Work* by The Verve
D. *The Wind in the Willows* by Kenneth Graham
E. Theme song from *Friends,* by The Rembrandts
F. First entry in the *British Telecom Birmingham Phone Book, 1988*

1...... 2...... 3......
4...... 5...... 6......

PICTURE OF HEAVEN

Draw your picture of heaven here:

SESSION 2: REVELATION 2 & 3

The Good, the Bad and the Struggling

◆ TEACHING POINT
These chapters show both what Jesus loves and hates to see in a church.

◆ GROUP AIM
For members to value what Jesus values in his people, and to avoid what he hates.

EQUIPMENT CHECKLIST *(Depending on which sections you tackle, you may need)*
- Flipchart or overhead projector
- Pens and paper
- Bibles
- Work-out sheets
- Lukewarm drinks
- Magazine pictures
- Mirror

LEADERS' GUIDE

Time doesn't allow us to study all seven letters thoroughly, although you might choose sometime to do a series of seven sessions. Several of the books listed on page 5 would be helpful if you decide to do that. We've provided here an overview activity or two and then a focus on the churches at Philadelphia (which Jesus unreservedly commends) and Laodicea (which receives his harsh criticism).

Don't let your members be put off by the names of the churches. They're not that hard to pronounce; they're just unfamiliar, that's all. Replace them if you like with Edinburgh, Stratford, Poole and others, just so long as the group focuses on what is being said to them by Jesus. The *Lion Handbook to the Bible* has a clear map of where the seven churches were, together with some photographs of how the towns and their ruins look now, which may help people to come to terms with hearing about unfamiliar places. If anyone has been to Turkey on holiday, get a map and see how near to the seven churches they went. They might be able to give an idea of what the countryside is like.

BIBLE BACKGROUND

Each letter begins with a reference to John's vision in chapter 1. (You could remind your members of what they found in *Saw, heard, did* in the first session.) Each letter ends with a marvellous promise. The gist of most of the promises is easy to grasp; they speak of God's lavish rewarding of his persevering people. So **Revelation 2:7,11** speaks of eternal life. The promise to Pergamum (**2:17**) is trickier. The manna may be most helpfully thought of as reminding us of the bread of life; the white stone cannot be definitely

SESSION 2

explained but clearly carries an assurance of blessing; the new name stands (in the thought of the times when John wrote) for a new character, bestowed by and known to God. In **2:26-28** those who overcome are promised authority and 'the Morning Star', which is Jesus himself (see **22:16**). A similar mixture of authority and the presence of Jesus is found in **3:21**. In **3:5** we have another promise of life, and reward for righteousness. The remaining promise, to the church in Philadelphia, is dealt with in the activity *What I need*, below.

Similarly, where Jesus highlights problems in the churches the trouble is generally pretty clear, at least in outline. However, some of the specifics are a bit obscure. The Nicolaitans (**2:6,15**), those who held to the teaching of Balaam (**2:14**) and Jezebel (**2:20**) probably all represent attempts to combine the form of Christianity with pagan practices and immorality. 'Satan's throne' (**2:13**) reflects the abundance and importance of pagan temples in Pergamum, especially in regard to the worship of the Roman emperor.

The best recommendation is probably not to spend too much time in speculation about these things, but to pick out the gist and move on.

➤ STARTING IT

Distinguishing marks
✪

If you're confident that no one will feel 'got at', ask if anyone in the group has any distinguishing marks, like moles, tattoos etc. Be honest about your own, especially if they're funny. Then ask what the group can remember from the vision of Jesus we looked at in the last session. Put these things on a flipchart or OHP and tick them off or add to them as you read the beginnings of the letters.

God-bothered
✪ ✪

Make a list together of things you think God dislikes seeing in his churches. Avoid back-biting about your own church.

In a nutshell
✪ ✪

Allocate one of the letters to each small group, pair or individual, depending on your numbers. If you don't have enough people, leave out the last two letters (to Philadelphia and Laodicea) because we'll look at them in more depth shortly. Ask people to read their letter and come up with one phrase to summarize the picture of that church that comes across. An example might be 'Ephesus: correct but cold'. Ask the groups to explain their phrase if need be. Match what has been found against the list you made in *God-bothered*. Bear in mind that God's list is a more reliable guide!

➤ TEACHING IT

Philadelphia story
✪ ✪ ✪

Input: along with Smyrna, this church has no fault pointed out (though its individual members must have been sinners like the rest of us). Smyrna was persevering under pressure; so, too, was Philadelphia, but more detail is given about the latter. Read **Revelation 3:1-7**.

PAGE 19

SESSION 2

Short on strength
✪ ✪

Ask people to act out some situations where people are inadequate for their jobs: an exhausted shot-putter, the Seventh Cavalry riding hamsters, Superman with a heavy cold, that sort of thing. You could do it as a game of charades, or just give people a topic and see what they come up with. Make the point that the Philadelphian church felt like this, but kept going (**3:8**).

What I need
✪ ✪ ✪

Share times when group members have been weak or ill. What did they feel in need of? Then give some input. The church in Philadelphia is promised the key things it needs. It has help (**3:8** – Jesus opening a door), reassurance (**3:9** – the certainty that they will be recognized as God's loved ones) and protection (**3:10** – their suffering will not be limitless). And their long-term reward will also be exactly suited to what weak, oppressed Christians need. They will have a crown, the status of a pillar (which is about as strong as you can be!), God's own presence, and the identification with God that comes from having God's own name written on them. All these can be found in **3:11-12**. In the light of this evidence of God's perfectly targeted help and blessing, have a short time when members can pray silently for what they feel they need.

On the other hand...
✪ ✪ ✪

By way of contrast, read Revelation **3:14-22**. Point out that the description of Jesus (**3:14**) means that this is a true and authoritative account. Pass round a few drinks of lukewarm coke, almost-cold coffee and so on. Most people would rather have the refreshment of real coldness or the luxury of warmth. Laodicea was near to some famous hot springs, but Jesus is saying that spiritually they have neither the pleasing effect of warmth, nor the brisk impact of coldness.

My mistake
✪

Give groups a few minutes to make up a skit, funny or not, about mistaken identity or situations. Give a prize for the one voted the best. Make the point that often the hardest thing is to be honest or realistic about ourselves. The Laodiceans had it wrong. They thought they were absolutely all right, but Jesus mercilessly exposes their shortcomings. What he offers them mirrors local conditions: they were very rich, had factories producing a lot of cloth and were famed for manufacturing eye ointment as well as other medicines. Despite these material advantages, their spiritual situation was desperate.

Two views
✪ ✪ ✪

Laodicea gives us a perfect picture of the world around us. Ask your group to suggest celebrities currently in the news, who seemed to have everything going for them but have turned out to have disastrous weaknesses or to be concealing

SESSION 2

terrible personal situations. Have some magazine pictures of suitable candidates ready. But then produce a mirror – the bigger the better – to replace the pictures. It's very easy to see these things in others, but not in ourselves. Laodicea would have had that problem. We need to beware of it in ourselves.

➤ DOING IT

Special offer
✪ ✪ ✪

Input: Jesus still offers great things to the Laodiceans, if they will repent (**3:18,21**). But they would have to accept the premise of **3:19**; that may not be too welcome to us, either. Allow a moment's silence for honest appraisal of that. In everything we need to 'overcome' (**3:21**, but also at the end of every letter). Discuss what that might mean in practice for members of your group.

Work-out
✪ ✪

Distribute copies of the Work-out sheet and ask members to delete bits and fill in the gaps for themselves, in line with how they think Jesus might see them. They should keep the sheet as a reminder.

Memory verse
✪ ✪ ✪

Revelation 3:21

'To him who overcomes, I will give the right to sit with me on my throne, just as I overcame and sat down with my Father on his throne.'

WORK-OUT

Jesus
1 Throne Road
Heaven

Dear ……………………………………

I'm *glad you are/sorry you are not* my follower.

You're one of the most *friendly/funky/fantastic/frantic* people I know, and I want to say *'Keep it up'/'Don't be afraid'/'I love you'*.

One of your great abilities is evidently ………………………………
You need to *make the most of this/stop doing this*.

People think of you as …………………………… Remember I can see the real you. I *like it/want to see some changes/am very sad about it*.

Of course, your church is *a great help/a resource you don't use as much as you should/not as much support as it should be,* but don't forget that I can supply *all the strength you need/an endless supply of unthreatening thrills/a safety net when everything else goes wrong*.

It would be great if you spoke to me soon about this. I look forward to hearing from you.

With a whole lot of love

Jesus

SESSION 3: REVELATION 4 & 5

Who Goes There?

◆ TEACHING POINT
Revelation's picture of God enthroned and Jesus returning to heaven in triumph transforms our view of our earthly circumstances.

◆ GROUP AIM
To worship Jesus afresh for what he has done for us.

EQUIPMENT CHECKLIST

(Depending on which sections you tackle, you may need)
- Copy of 'Breaking into Heaven' from the album *Second Coming* by the Stone Roses
- VCR, TV and appropriate film previews
- Jewellery
- Overhead projector or flipchart and pens
- A padlock and a load of keys
- Video collage
- Copies of *The Alternative Service Book* (1980)

LEADERS' GUIDE

After the practical, pastoral wisdom of the previous two chapters we arrive at the all-encompassing wisdom of our vision of heaven. Worship the Lamb! Revelation is going to teach us a lot about worship. In particular, we are going to see that a large part of the activity of heaven involves such worship. We need to make it clear to our groups that the often inadequate worship that takes place in some of our churches is but a small and partial insight into heavenly worship.

We need to offer this warning in case our members are tempted to say, 'Well, if heaven is like church services I don't want to go.' Frankly, we wouldn't want to go either. But just occasionally, Christian worship takes us out of ourselves and into the presence of God; heavenly worship is like that always, only better. Wow!

BIBLE BACKGROUND

After the letters to the seven churches we have, almost, a new start. A door opens (**4:1**) and John proceeds into the rest of the vision. Again he refers to himself as 'in the Spirit' (**4:2**) as he did in **1:10**. This indicates a change. John has been writing down the precise words of God to the seven churches. Now he is seeing the opening scene in a picture of future events.

Revelation 4 concerns God the Creator – the One on the throne; **Revelation 5:1-11** presents the Redeemer – the Lamb who was slain. John records a hymn of praise (**5:12-14**), sung by everyone, to the One on the throne and the Lamb. Father and Son are equal recipients of our praises.

The throne (**4:2-6**). God the Creator has been watching the unfolding of human drama and history, yet is somehow distant from it too. Doing the best

SESSION 3

he can within the limitations of human language, John presents a picture of being in the presence of the Father. Here are the finest precious stones (**4:3**), the cleanest of clean robes (**4:4**) and the most dramatic of exciting weather conditions (**4:5**). This is an awesome place to be.

It is surrounded by twenty-four elders. Most good commentaries offer their own interpretation of the symbolic function of those whose purpose seems to be primarily worship. Since there are twelve apostles, twelve tribes, twelve Babylonian star-gods and twenty-four priestly Levitical orders, those who enjoy juggling with numbers have had a field day. There are also twenty-four letters in the English alphabet if you don't count the first and the last; don't let it worry you. You can do anything with numbers if you work at it for long enough.

The creatures (**4:6b-11**). Lion, ox, eagle and human being represent the mightiest of wild animals, domestic animals and birds, with human beings as the pinnacle of creation and mightiest of all.

Revelation 5 describes the triumph and uniqueness of Christ. He alone is worthy to open the seals and take us on into the vision of the last things in Revelation 6 and the following chapters. Among the titles and attributes of Jesus in the chapter is 'the Lion of the tribe of Judah, the Root of David' (**5:5**). This is formed from two Old Testament texts, both of which were thought to point to the Messiah: they are **Genesis 49:9** and **Isaiah 11:1**.

➤ STARTING IT

'Breaking into heaven' ✪

Introduce the whole session by playing 'Breaking into Heaven' from the Stone Roses' second album *Second Coming*. It's eleven minutes long, so have a game or refreshments at the same time.

Try brainstorming how many references to heaven your group can think of from contemporary music.

Preview ✪ ✪

Many videos have a short opening section previewing upcoming films – and that guy with the wonderfully deep voice narrating almost all of them. They get you excited about forthcoming video releases. Find a suitable set to play to your group and ask them which of the previewed films they want to see.

Revelation 4 is a preview of **Revelation 5** where we will meet the person of Christ once again; the One who 'is worthy to break the seals and open the scroll'. But the focus is sharpened by having to wait. Read chapter 4 and brainstorm how members feel concerning the events that are described. What do they feel they are waiting for?

Point out that chapter 4 concerns God as Creator, but chapter 5 will focus on God as Redeemer (and therefore Jesus).

SESSION 3

Jeweller ✪

If you live somewhere convenient, take your group on a walk into a shopping area where there is a jeweller. (If you are meeting outside shopping hours, check first that they leave goods on display.) Identify some precious stones and metals. You will probably see gold, silver, diamonds, emeralds, sapphires and rubies. Explain the jewels found in the passage:

jasper – red, yellow or brown opaque quartz
carnelian – red quartz
emerald – bright green stone

Alternatively, invite some parents to bring along their jewellery to show to the group. Read **4:1-6**.

➤ TEACHING IT

Worship brainstorm 1 ✪ ✪ ✪

It has been said that every word of **Revelation 4** is designed to give glory to the Creator. Check it out. Read the passage and list on a flipchart or acetate all the words that tell us something about the Creator. Your list might include:

Enthroned **(4:2)**   Magnificent **(4:3)**   Awesome **(4:5)**   Holy **(4:8)**
Worshipped **(4:8)**   Eternal **(4:8-9)**   Worthy **(4:11)**   Creator **(4:11)**

When complete, take a few moments to pray thankfully and quietly, using your word-list as a visual aid.

Open the lock ✪ ✪

Write 'Only the one who is worthy can open the lock' on a piece of paper and seal it in an envelope. Get hold of a padlock and hide its key. Bring along a selection of other keys. Place the selection of 'wrong' keys in front of the group and pass round the padlock. Let them take turns in trying to open it.

When all have had a go, give someone the sealed envelope. Ask them to open it and read the message.

Hopefully your group will now have the same sense of frustration as John had at the start of **Revelation 5**, although they will probably not have resorted to tears. Read **Revelation 5**.

Something nice ✪

If you want to have an interesting discussion with more able groups, have a second envelope handy containing a promise of something nice: lemonade, chocolate biscuits, a lift home for everyone.

Having read it aloud, ask what the status of the promise was before it had been read out.

Make the connection. The Gospels and other New Testament writings assure us of salvation through Jesus Christ. **Revelation 5** is a picture of this salvation

SESSION 3

being worked out. But the assurance (in **John 3:16**, for instance) of eternal life for the believer was there beforehand.

Worship brainstorm 2

Read **Revelation 5**. List the pictures and attributes of Jesus. For example:

The Lion of the tribe of Judah, the Root of David (**5:5**)
Triumphed (**5:5**)
A Lamb, looking as if it had been slain (**5:6**)
The subject of our songs of worship (**5:9**)
Worthy (**5:9**)

When complete, again take a few moments to pray thankfully and quietly, using your word-list as a visual aid.

Ceremonial video

Revelation 5 describes an enthronement ceremony. It is also a victory ceremony. It would be excellent if you could put together a video collage of various human events. How about including:

Soldiers disembarking after a victory in battle
The FA Cup being held aloft
The enthronement of a king or queen
The Oscar presentation for best film.

Point out that Jesus won the battle over sin and death on the cross and now comes to the throne to claim his rightful place. Read **Revelation 5:13-14**.

➤ DOING IT

Worship

Again, the best response is worship. Many modern choruses pick up the words of **Revelation 4 & 5**. The canticle 'Glory and Honour' (*The Alternative Service Book 1980*, page 67) is also based on the passage. Use some incense sticks to pick up the imagery in **5:8**.

Memory verse

Try and learn **Revelation 5:12**.
'Worthy is the Lamb, who was slain, to receive power and wealth and wisdom and strength and honour and praise!'

Earthsong

The vision of heaven is there not for its own sake but to draw out a changed view of earthly circumstances. How has this session changed the way members of your group see their lives now? Ask them.

Amen

The last two verses of Revelation 5 offer an 'Amen'. This translates as 'so be it', or to put it more simply, 'Yes!' When we say 'Amen' we say yes to all that God has done for us in Christ. Bring along a supply of painting, drawing and decorating materials and invite members to spend a few minutes making an ornate 'Amen' using the Work-out sheet. Display the results.

PAGE 26

NEW AMEN

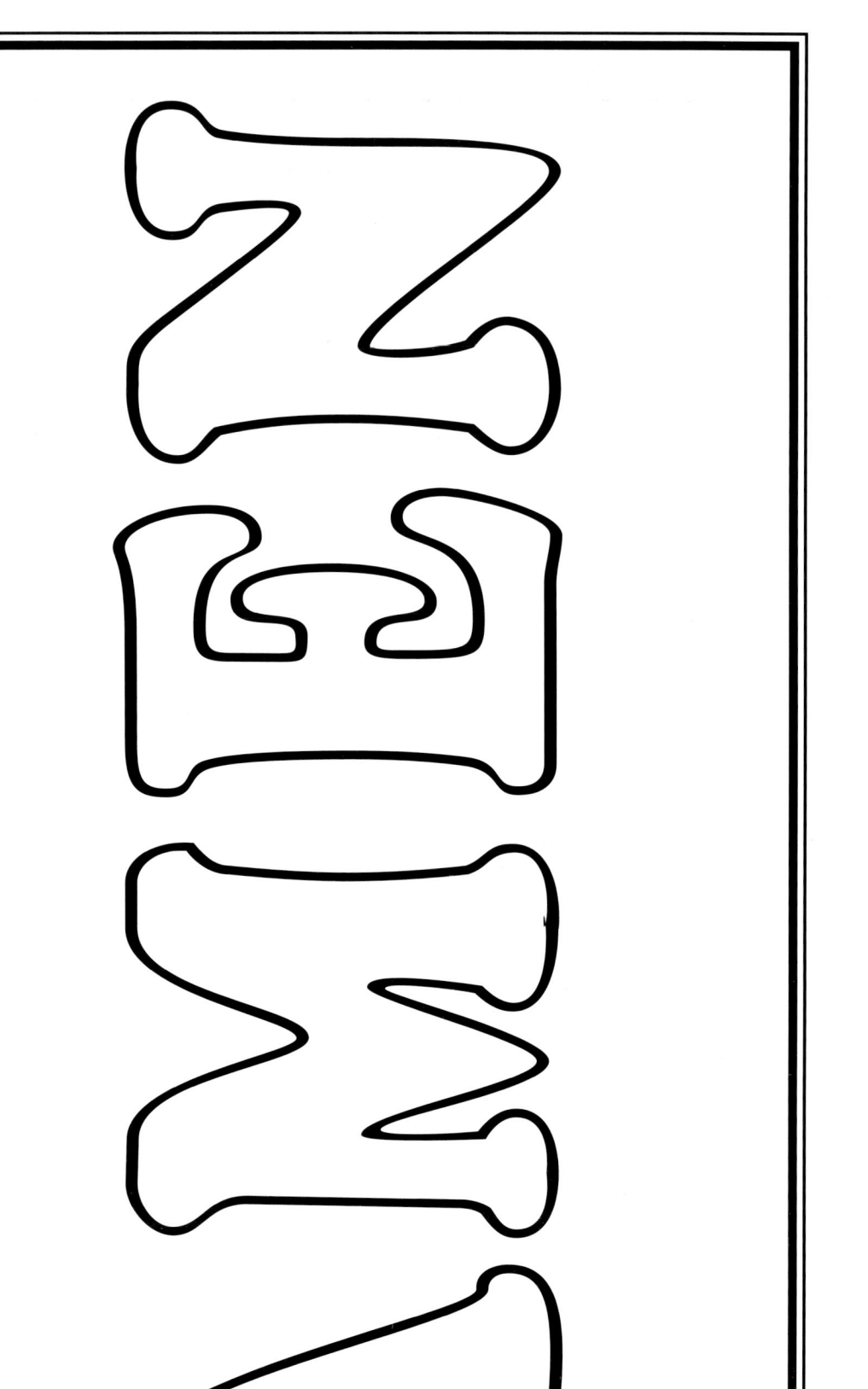

WORK-OUT

SESSION 4: REVELATION 6:1 - 8:5

Shelter from the Storm

◆ TEACHING POINT
Judgement and salvation go together.

◆ GROUP AIM
For members to understand fully the horror from which Jesus rescues us.

EQUIPMENT CHECKLIST

(Depending on which sections you tackle, you may need)
- Bibles
- Pens and paper
- Loud music
- Wrapped chocolates
- Material about suffering Christians
- Work-out sheets (cut up in advance)
- Wood, hammer and nails
- Sheets and paint
- The game Jenga
- Flipchart or overhead projector
- Incense stick

LEADERS' GUIDE

We're in the swing of it now; you'll recognize in this passage similarities and themes in common with session 3, and that will continue to be true in future passages and sessions. Encourage the group to identify these – the study of Revelation will be of far more use to them if they remember the big themes than if they concentrate on individual details. Perhaps you could delegate a group member to keep a list of themes which come up week by week, to help the group keep track of the main thrust of the book.

In preparing for this session, it will be helpful to get some information about Christians around the world who are being oppressed and even martyred. This links with the *High five* activity and will lend it more impact. The following are all possible sources of such information:

Keston Institute
4 Park Town, OXFORD OX2 6SH
Tel: (01865) 311022
E-mail: keston.institute@keston.org

Amnesty International
1 Easton Street, LONDON WC1X 8DJ
Tel: (0171) 956 1157

Open Doors with Brother Andrew
PO Box 6, WITNEY OX8 7SP
Tel: (01865) 300262/300223
E-mail: 106333.1732@compuserve.com

SESSION 4

In your preparation time, use the scenes of judgement in this passage to inform your view of God, and the scenes of worship to kick-start your own praise. Revelation can and should feed us as much as our group members!

☞ BIBLE BACKGROUND

The four riders at the beginning of chapter 6 portray different aspects of God's judgement. Bear in mind that a horse then was a symbol of power and military strength; perhaps if this vision were given today it would involve an armoured personnel carrier or a fighter plane! You may need to bring the bow (**Revelation 6:2**) and sword (**6:4**) similarly up to date to give the group an idea of the power of God that is being portrayed.

Seals one, two and four unleash conquest, warfare, strife and miscellaneous horrors. The third seal is the most obscure. It refers to economic hardship, with the necessities of everyday life costing all the money that most people earn, but luxuries still available for the rich.

As throughout Revelation – and the rest of the Bible – stark pictures of the fate of those who are not among God's people are contrasted with the ultimate joy of those who are. The last three verses of chapter 6 offer a shocking contrast to the scenes of worship in the second half of chapter 7.

The tribes and numbers in **7:4-8** should not be taken literally in this book full of symbolism. Jehovah's Witnesses take the 144,000 literally, but not the reference to their all being from Jewish tribes, nor that their reappearance in chapter 14 shows them all to be male and, probably, virgins. Other sects take different parts of the vision literally, but the message John wants to convey is that all God's people will be brought to safety in him, and none lost. There are twelve tribes of Israel; there are twelve apostles. Twelve is one of the 'perfect' numbers in Revelation. Multiplying twelve by twelve and then by one thousand, which is a number signifying greatness, is symbolic of God's full salvation.

➤ STARTING IT

Culture shock
✪ ✪

Play some (very) loud music, with people shouting along, and then, at a pre-arranged signal, have silence. Or you could have a group hug, then suddenly break off into threatening gestures. Explain that we're dealing with that kind of sudden shift at the beginning of this passage. Remind people what happened at the end of chapter 5 and then read chapter 6.

Choc shock
✪ ✪

Change the wrappings in order to disguise a number of familiar small chocolates. Ask people to guess what each might be, and link this to the opening of the different seals in chapter 6: we come to realize in general terms what's coming, but not the precise contents. Allow people to open a few chocolates from time to time as you go through the session.

Just deserts
✪ ✪ ✪

Ask the group to name some current or recent high-profile court cases. Point out that wherever there is right and wrong, there must be judgement and

SESSION 4

punishment. Here in Revelation we are spectators as that principle is demonstrated; the seven seals signify that this is judgement in its fullness. Talk through the first four seals with the group. We can see these things happening (bar the horses) in the world already. Is God's judgement already at work in the way we treat each other, without our realizing?

Seals five to seven show the future judgement. As well as working now, God is going to finish his work of judgement at a time of his choosing. Give everyone a 'part one' from the Work-out sheet and see if anyone can guess what the final picture will be. Then give 'part two' and so on. Keep going until everyone knows what they have.

Remind people that although we see some of God's work now, we won't get the full picture in this life.

➤ TEACHING IT

High five
✪ ✪ ✪

Look together at some material about Christians currently suffering for their faith. How would your group feel if armed police suddenly burst in to your meeting and beat people up or dragged them off? Would your members turn up again for next week's meeting? Remind them of the memory verse from session 2 (**Revelation 3:21**), and read **Revelation 2:10**. Then read again the verses about the fifth seal. Point out the text's note of yearning – longing for God to come and tie up all the loose ends. Make a list together of things your members wish that God would come and deal with or put an end to. Read 6:11 – we need to persevere and have patience, trusting God's purposes. The Church will have to suffer while God makes his people and his kingdom perfect.

Big bang
✪ ✪

Get some bits of wood, a hammer and some nails. Allow everybody seven hammer blows and see who can get a nail farthest into the wood. Be careful of what's underneath! Recap on the seven seals. The overall effect is like seven hammer blows; they're all working towards the same end.

Pretty pictures
✪

Provide some old bed sheets (from generous church members or from charity shops) and paint, and get the group to create one or more banners illustrating **Revelation 6:12-17**. See if you can arrange for the banners to be displayed in church: they'll make a change from doves in pastel shades, and will give a strong biblical message for congregation and visitors.

The in-crowd
✪ ✪ ✪

You could repeat *Culture shock* from the beginning of the session, to mark the transition at the beginning of chapter 7. Read the chapter. Savour it! Explain about

PAGE 30

SESSION 4

the tribes and the numbers (see Bible Background), and that the number heard is symbolic: the uncountable multitude is the reality. A similar symbolic number and uncountable crowd can be found in **Revelation 9:16-17**.

Bow down

Have a time of worship, celebrating chapter 7. Your worship doesn't have to be singing – give your members a chance to respond in ways they feel comfortable with, whether musical, artistic, silent, spoken, active or whatever. If you're stuck for ideas, we're happy to recommend *DIY Worship,* from CPAS, which is stacked with ideas and useful accessories. Ring the number on page 63 of this book to find out more.

Shock more

You could also repeat *Culture shock* here, to mark the abrupt silence at the beginning of chapter 8. Or you could have a half-hour silence if you've the time. Sponsorship makes it more likely that a room full of teenagers will manage it. Help people to understand that this is not the silence of boredom, but of awed anticipation. It's a bit like when we're reduced to whispering at a truly wonderful sight, only more so, or the tense silence when we're wondering if the Jenga tower is about to fall down. Verse 5 is when the tower falls. Why not play Jenga and make that point?

➤ DOING IT

Count me in?

Ask people to sum up the qualification for taking part in the heavenly praise session of chapter 7. Write the suggestions up, and if necessary add in the need to be servants of God (**6:3**) and, surprise surprise, to persevere (**6:14**). Have a time (less than half an hour) of silence for people to assess themselves against these criteria.

Pray

Have a time of open prayer, geared to the confidence and maturity of your group. If you don't suffer from smoke alarms, have an incense stick or some other reminder of the censer in **8:3** to symbolize the prayers ascending to God. You may have to explain the difference between a censer and a censor, or use a version such as the *Good News Bible* which uses a different word.

Memory verse

Revelation 7:10
And they cried out in a loud voice: 'Salvation belongs to our God, who sits on the throne, and to the Lamb.'

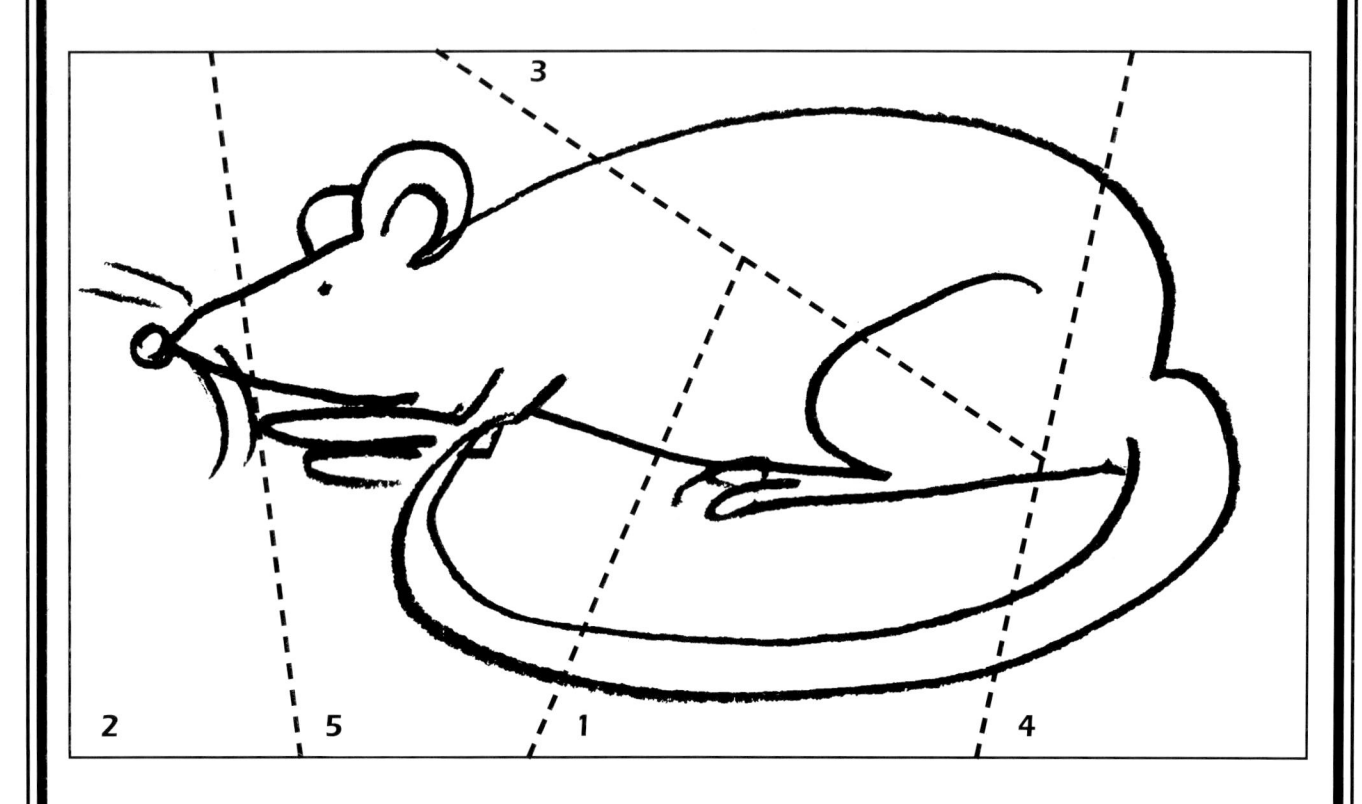

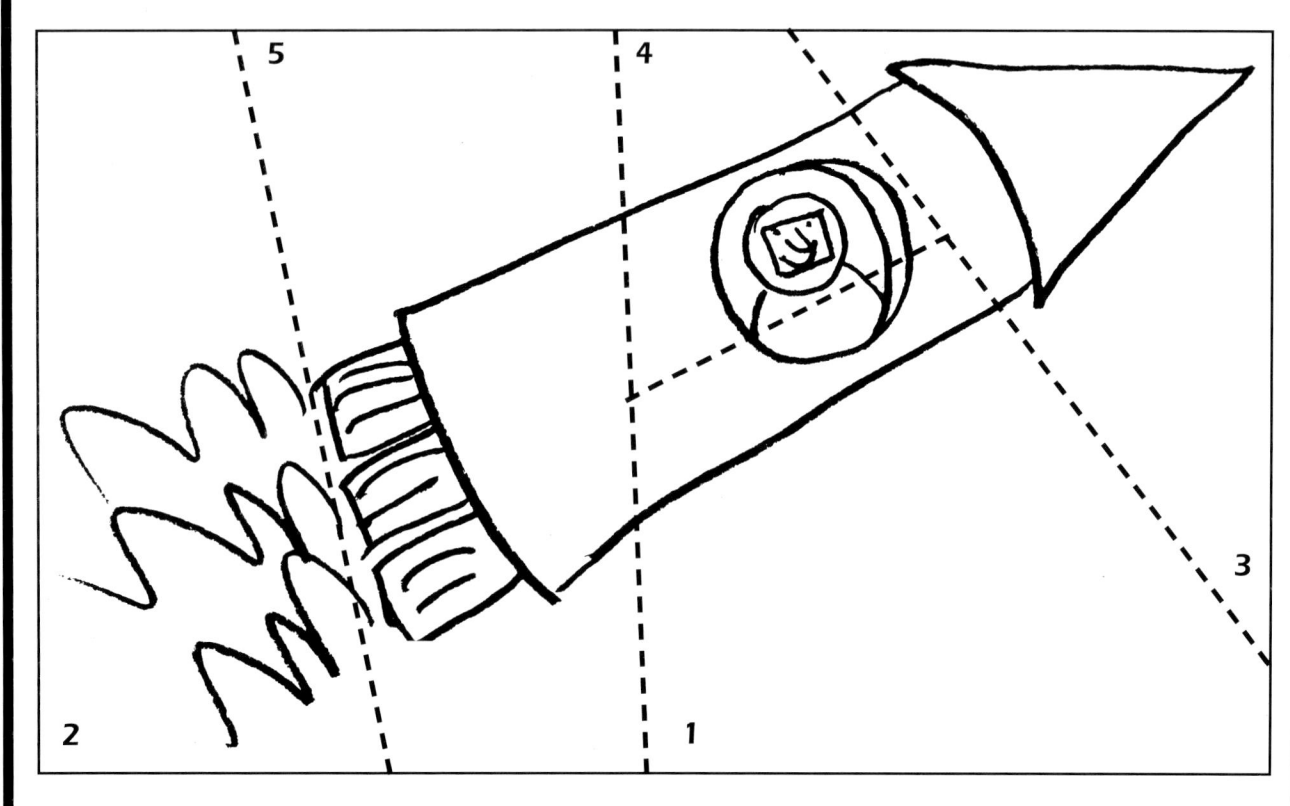

WORK-OUT

SESSION 5: REVELATION 8:6 - 11:18

Environmental Health

◆ TEACHING POINT
There is a correct Christian attitude towards the world and our stewardship of it. This attitude involves both turning to Christ and halting exploitative practices.

◆ GROUP AIM
That the group should come to repentance for their misuse of some scarce resources and should pray for the health of the planet.

EQUIPMENT CHECKLIST

(Depending on which sections you tackle, you may need)
- Bibles or copies of the passage
- Honey, lemon and ginger drinks
- A trumpet or bugle (and trumpeter/bugler if necessary)
- Flipchart or overhead projector
- A sliced lemon and some sugar lumps
- Copies of the Work-out sheet, pencils and some envelopes
- Some ambient music

LEADERS' GUIDE

The middle chapters of Revelation do tend to labour the same point. In chapters 8 to 11 we are not primarily concerned with the environment. The material is about the disruption of nature brought about by God as judgement on humankind for sin, rather than humankind as the cause of environmental disorder. These four chapters include desperate and horrible judgement statements. We must beware of scaremongering.

You might like to explain to your group that, while environmental issues are not the main theme of these chapters (judgement is) you are going to take the opportunity to think about the environment, and environmental sins in particular, in order to anticipate God's judgement in this area.

Yet if we are to take them seriously we must do a rather difficult balancing act:

1. We must accept that we have spoiled the world. We have, as individuals, played a part in the deterioration of the environment. We need to repent and try to find ways of behaving appropriately towards the environment.

2. We must accept that people will not come to a sensible attitude towards God's world until they come to faith in God. Therefore evangelism is just as valid a response to a decaying planet as are issues of 'green' farming.

A good conclusion to this session would be for your members to agree to pray for their friends *and* drop less litter.

SESSION 5

☞ BIBLE BACKGROUND

We have a trumpeter in our church music group. His is the only instrument in the group that doesn't need amplifying. It makes, ahem, a hell of a racket.

The sounding of trumpets can signify all sorts of things – the beginning of a royal wedding perhaps, or the movement of an army. Although other places in the New Testament identify trumpets as 'raising the dead' (see **1 Corinthians 15:52**), we must be careful. In chapter 1 the noise John first heard was like the sounding of a trumpet. The trumpet signifies that something special is about to happen.

Seven trumpets. Each of the first four signifies judgement on some state of the world that is not being stewarded in accordance with God's plan for it:

1. (**8:7**) agriculture and countryside
2. (**8:8-9**) cities and commerce
3. (**8:10-11**) rivers and seas
4. (**8:12**) light.

The fifth, sixth and seventh trumpets are somewhat different:

5. (**9:1-12**) When people do not accept Christ, the Bible's clear teaching is that they are choosing death rather than life. The fifth trumpet makes clear that any way other than the way of Christ is the way of torment. There is a connection between illness, suffering and sin. In a fallen world the connection is not as clearly defined as some would say. The question, 'What have I done to deserve this?' is rarely capable of a one-word answer.

6. (**9:13-21**) If suffering points people to God, then how much more should death and bereavement? One thing that should stir people into faith is the death of people who have no faith. What will become of them? The sixth trumpet has been sounding loudly since Christ ascended; put your faith in him before you die.

There is a pause between trumpets six and seven. It is a representative pause. The first six trumpets have indicated the travail of the world. The seventh will indicate final judgement. In between there are messages, scrolls, worship, prophecy and preaching. In the midst of the travail of the present age it is the Church's, and therefore our, job to spread the gospel.

7. (**11:15-18**) The final trumpet signals the end. God has offered people every opportunity to repent. He would offer further, but the human capacity to respond has gone. If the first six trumpets do not make a difference, then that is it. It brings to mind the words of Jesus: 'If they do not listen to Moses and the Prophets, they will not be convinced even if someone rises from the dead' (**Luke 16:31**).

As ever, it would be helpful if there was some way your group could read, or

SESSION 5

listen to, all four chapters. However, we will concentrate on the first four trumpets in **Revelation 8**, on the need to share our faith (key verse **10:7**) and on our need, as Christians, to respond with gratitude for our salvation from such violent judgement (**11:15-18**).

➤ STARTING IT

Blow your own trumpet
✪

Get hold of a trumpet and ask a succession of volunteers to try and get a note out of it. If there is someone in your group who can play, ask them to demonstrate. It is a difficult instrument to learn.

If you want a really loud noise, contact your local Boys' Brigade or British Legion and borrow a bugler.

Read **Revelation 8:2,6-7a**.

What's wrong?
✪ ✪ ✪

On a flipchart or overhead projector, list 'global-scale' things that are wrong with the world. If necessary start the ball rolling by mentioning declining fish stocks, sweat-shop industries, fields used to produce drugs instead of food – and so on.

Read **Revelation 8:7-12**.

Honey and lemon
✪

Lead people into the sweet and sour nature of **Revelation 10:9-11** by having honey and lemon drinks instead of your usual refreshments.

Put a teaspoonful of thick honey and a tablespoonful of lemon into a mug. Pour on boiling water and stir until the honey dissolves. Good for colds. Add some ginger if you really want to get some air down your nose.

➤ TEACHING IT

Then and now
✪ ✪ ✪

Explain that some people talk of the picture language in **Revelation 8:7-12** as descriptive of that which will happen just before Jesus comes again. We take the view that a better understanding is that it is descriptive of the problems of the planet as they have *always* been.

If you did the brainstorm *What's wrong?* at the beginning of the session, look back at the list.

See if you can group the items under the headings represented by the first six trumpets. Take a moment to pray quietly as you look at the list and perhaps to use a confessional prayer.

SESSION 5

Repent
✪ ✪

Take a lemon and cut it into slices. Give them to two or three 'volunteers'. After a few moments of sucking and face pulling, offer the volunteers a sugar lump. Ask them to describe the experience.

Input from leader time:

Read **Revelation 10:7**. There is continuity between that which the prophets spoke and that which will come to pass.

Read **Revelation 10:8-11**. In 'the last days' (the time between Jesus' ascension and his coming again) it remains, right up to the last minute, our responsibility to preach/share the gospel. **Jude 23** talks about snatching people from the fire. That is dramatic language. Our response to the gospel involves heart-rending responsibilities and consequences: someone converted from an Islamic background may be disowned by their family. But on our tongues, as we see people converted by its power, the gospel is sweet.

My private prayer list
✪ ✪ ✪

Use the list on the Work-out sheet to get members thinking about their family/friends and the gospel.

Encourage them to look forward to the day when 'the time has come for rewarding ... those who reverence your name'(**Revelation 11:18**).

Why not place the sheets in envelopes, collect them and agree to give them back in, say, six months. Then further prayer can take place and, perhaps, some rejoicing.

➤ DOING IT

What can I do?
✪ ✪

The problems of the global environment seem very distant to us. Spend some time discussing things that your group can do to make a difference:

Clean up a street
Buy fairly traded goods from organizations such as Traidcraft
Walk or cycle more

Covenant together to put one or two of these into practice.

Thanks be to God
✪ ✪ ✪

Reread **Revelation 11:15-18**, perhaps over some ambient, instrumental music and lead into a time of open prayer and praise.

WORK-OUT

MY PRIVATE PRAYER LIST

Christian friends and family (that they might stay faithful)

....

....

....

....

....

....

....

Friends who I believe might respond to Jesus

....

....

....

....

Those for whom it would take a miracle

....

....

....

....

SESSION 6: REVELATION 11:19 - 14:13

Filth Sandwich

◆ TEACHING POINT
The blood of the Lamb and the word of testimony must be our focus.

◆ GROUP AIM
For members to distinguish between true and counterfeit religion.

EQUIPMENT CHECKLIST

(Depending on which sections you tackle, you may need)
- Bibles
- Pens and paper
- Customized cake
- Nice cake
- *Silence of the Lambs* video
- Playing cards
- Arty things

LEADERS' GUIDE

Why 'Filth Sandwich', then? Because chapter 12 and the first half of chapter 14 describe the triumph of the forces of heaven; in the middle is the foul picture of the temporary success of Satan's counterfeit religion.

Two great sequences of judgement have gone; one is to come. But this interlude, like the end of chapter 11, is not all sweetness and light. In fact, although we're at a new 'opening' (**11:19**), we are still linked to the end of the second sequence, watching the working out of the arrival of God's kingdom. There is loads of symbolism in this section from different parts of Middle Eastern mythology, drawn together to show God's supremacy over all such systems.

And we're afloat in a sea of symbols now. Those who want to can make whatever they like of the individual pictures, so we must make sure we know the flow of the plot! For example, **12:1** could be straight out of New Age thinking, but is also reminiscent of Joseph's dream in **Genesis 37:9** and so points us to the woman's key place in the history of God's rescue of his people.

BIBLE BACKGROUND

This section deals with the great challenge of demonic 'religion', aping the real thing. We need to start by thinking about 'signs'. In John's Gospel, Jesus' miracles are called signs – they point to the reality of who he is. The same word is used here in verses **12:1** and **12:3**, with regard to the appearance of the woman and the dragon. Just as in the rest of John's vision, we're not dealing with literal, physical events here, but with pictures pointing to a spiritual reality.

Not all signs, though, point to the truth. They can be instruments of deception,

SESSION 6

as in **13:3** and **13:13-14**. The test for whether signs and wonders are from God must be taken from **12:11**. Are they witnessing to the blood of the Lamb (Jesus' work on the cross) by their testimony?

The sea is an important symbol in Revelation, and stands for the turbulent rebellion of people and nations against God's rule. Note that when his kingdom is fully established there is 'no longer any sea' (**21:1**).

Numbers come flying at us in this section like a lottery draw. Most of them can be interpreted under the rule that seven is a 'perfect' number and anything less is imperfect. So the evil forces have complete worldly strength, but their rule is incomplete (1260 days and 42 months both = three-and-a-half years, 'a time, times and half a time' = three-and-a-half ages). Twelve is the other perfect number, and applies here to the woman (**12:1**) and the saved (see the Bible Background on the 144,000 in chapter 7). Ten is a number of 'greatness' (and the various multiples of 1000 that crop up through the book are correspondingly greater). The number of the beast almost certainly is a coded reference to one of the Roman emperors, by allocating a numerical value to each letter of the name according to its place in the alphabet. In English, the name 'Ian' could have a coded value of 9+1+14=24. The emperor is probably Nero, although as is usual with Revelation, there are rival theories. The most persuasive is that 6 is 'the human number' because mankind was created on the sixth day: therefore the number 666 stands for man trying to be God.

The woman of **12:1** represents the people of God, the community from which comes the Messiah (represented here by her child). Michael is the angelic champion of God's people, appearing also in **Daniel 10 & 12** and **Jude 9**. Let's remember, though, that the key to salvation is not Michael's intervention and a whirl of heavenly fireworks but 'the blood of the Lamb'.

One item in this section about which people get very worried is the 'mark of the beast' (**13:16-18**). Given the way God's people are said to be sealed or marked in **7:3** and **14:1**, attempts to identify this with a physical mark seem way off beam. It's a matter of who you follow, not who tattoos, brands, paints or tags you.

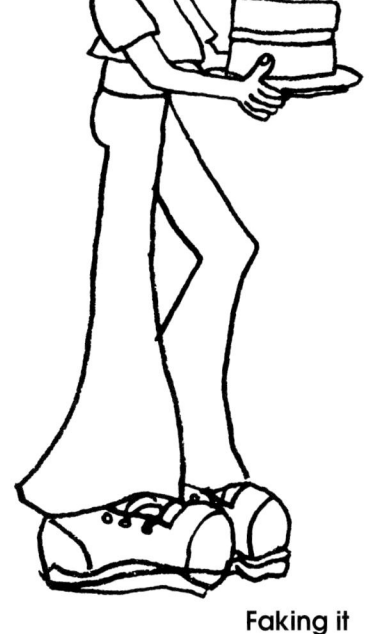

➤ STARTING IT

Faking it
✪ ✪ ✪

Make, or get some friendly member of the congregation to make for you, a luscious-looking cake containing a hefty dose of chilli powder or other unpleasant ingredient. Offer slices around and see the reaction. It would be kind to have some glasses of water available, though you may end up wearing their contents – so take care. Ask if the shock was worse because people were expecting something sweet and pleasant. Explain that that's what we're focusing on in this session. Put the Work-out sheet onto acetate

PAGE 39

SESSION 6

and use it on an OHP to give an overview of this passage. It would be really good to have a proper, extra-delicious cake for later on.

Yuk ✪

Show a video clip from *Silence of the Lambs*; select the scene in which Hannibal Lecter disguises himself with someone else's face, and then reveals himself. We're dealing here with loathsome people being unmasked.

You've been framed ✪ ✪

Ask the group to contribute examples of times when they've been taken in by someone. How did they find out that they had been duped?

➤ TEACHING IT

Get stuck in ✪ ✪

Have a bit of an arm-wrestling contest, or a game of snap or some other highly competitive activity. Then read chapter 12, encouraging people as they listen to spot the different conflicts that take place. Ask if they think they can identify the woman and her child. Give an explanation if necessary. Point out that even when the dragon knows he has been defeated he still fights hard, cunningly and with great power, symbolized by his heads, horns and crowns. We can never take him lightly.

I like that ✪ ✪ ✪

Discuss what things impress the members of your group. Money? Power? Glamorous lifestyles? The gift of the gab? Humour? Then ask if these things translate into church life – or do other things impress us in high-profile Christians? It's dangerous to be too impressed by outward appearances or conspicuous talents, as personality can become more important to us than the truth. Read **12:10-12** again. What is the most important thing (or things) a Christian can have or do, according to these verses? In **12:11** there is a threefold answer: trusting in Jesus' death on the cross, witnessing to that and – as a summary – persevering (that word again!) in all circumstances.

Spitting image ✪ ✪ ✪

Enjoy or endure some group members doing impressions of singers, TV personalities, your minister and so on. Then read chapter 13. We're in the counterfeit zone now. Make a list together of ways in which the devil and his minions are seen to deceive people. Be sure to include people claiming to be Jesus (as with the 'lamb-alike' of **13:11**). Then take a few minutes to draw up a poster, warning people against the devil's deceptions. It's important we should all be warned – the deceit is aimed at 'normal' people, not just spiritual superstars.

Oo-er ✪ ✪

These verses (**13:16-18**) are a rich source of well-meaning but zany speculation. Read them together and ask if your members have any idea to what the mark or the beast's number refer. Encourage them not to lose any sleep over it. At the least, though, the mark is a reminder to check any mass commercial and cultural movements against biblical principles. It's easier to go with the flow, but plainly Christians may have to suffer financially for sticking to God's ways. See the Bible Background for information about the beast's number.

PAGE 40

SESSION 6

Back to reality

✪ ✪ ✪

Input: just as the villain seems to have won the day, in leaps the hero! Suddenly we look up and see the real, the true. It puts all the counterfeit stuff into perspective. Read **14:1-5**. This is Jesus and his people, in worship and strength. Ask the group to recall from chapter 7 who the 144,000 are; **14:4-5** shows them to be utterly pure, true and precious to God. Have a moment's silence to meditate on this.

Three angels

✪

The angels give a message about God and his opponents (**14:6-13**). Ask the group, working in pairs, and before reading the angels' messages, to come up with a news headline on this theme. We'll meet Babylon (**14:8**) again later. The message of God's victory and judgement should be no surprise by now. Nor should the refrain found in **13:10** and **14:12**.

➤ DOING IT

Memory verse

✪ ✪ ✪

Revelation 14:12
This calls for patient endurance on the part of the saints who obey God's commandments and remain faithful to Jesus.

Stand-up slot

✪

In the light of the need to resist false religion and ungodly ways, and the call to persevere and witness to the truth, ask people to think of specific ways in which they might make a stand for Jesus in the week ahead. If it's appropriate for your group, share these ways with one another.

Pray

✪ ✪

Use the suggestions on the Work-out sheet, or just do it in whatever way suits the group, but make some use of the themes and words of worship found in chapters 12 and 14, and bear in mind the thoughts people had in *Stand-up slot*.

WORK-OUT

WHAT'S GOING ON?

STEP 1
There's a fight going on!
There's a lot of action, but we haven't seen the end of it yet.

STEP 2
A couple of beasts seem to have won!
They offer great power and miraculous abilities! Are they good news?

STEP 3
They weren't good news. Now we see the real winner –
the Lamb is stronger than the beasts! His power is real and lasts for ever.
That's good news!

We pray against...
- all the false versions of religion that put us or others above God
- giving in to thinking that our happiness is more important than honouring God
- the persecution and oppression of our Christian brothers and sisters

Thank you, God, for...
- those who help us to understand your word
- those who set a godly example for us to follow
- the knowledge of your certain victory over evil powers
- the knowledge that you're strong enough to save us in the end

SESSION 7: REVELATION 14:14 - 16:21

Time, Everyone, Please!

◆ TEACHING POINT
God is patient, but not infinitely patient. There will be a judgement.

◆ GROUP AIM
For members to understand where they must put their trust when it comes to judgement.

EQUIPMENT CHECKLIST

(Depending on which sections you tackle, you may need)
- Masking tape
- 20 postcards
- Copy of 'Calling All Avenging Angels' by Space
- *Raiders of the Lost Ark* video
- Prints/posters of well-known paintings
- Slips of paper with verses on them
- Post-it notes and some loud music

LEADERS' GUIDE

Babylonian splattering. Now there's an unpleasant thought. Unpleasant for us, that is. At the end of **Psalm 137** the Psalmist rejoices in the idea of smashing the heads of Babylonian children against rocks. Not a happy bunny, then?

Well, no. But we need to beware of replacing the word 'Babylonian' with our own particular villains of the day: Iraq; the IRA; Islamic fundamentalists. That's not how it's meant to work.

In this session we have a powerful picture of the judgement coming on God's enemies. God's special people (the Jews) had suffered at the hands of an occupying (Roman) army in their own land and many Christians were now being persecuted for their faith. The passages in this session begin to answer the question, 'How long must this continue?' It is therefore a passage with which persecuted Christians everywhere today will identify.

BIBLE BACKGROUND

This passage is about judgement. Please try and teach the passage. It would be easy to read it and then teach everything you know about judgement, but that would be to miss this passage's unique contribution to Scripture.

Commentaries place **Revelation 14:14-20** at the end of the series of seven visions of conflict between the Church and evil powers (starting at **11:19**). They then disagree about whether **15:1-4** ends that series of visions (Wilcock/Richardson) or begins the next (Beasley-Murray/Morris). Why have we started where we have?

First for the simple, practical reason of trying to avoid taking too big a chunk of Revelation at a time. Secondly because there is a close link between the

SESSION 7

harvest of the earth, which leaves bloody carnage (**14:14-20**), and the seven bowls of final judgement which are described next (**15:1 - 16:21**). These passages should not be viewed as chronological but as a sharper focus on the same thing – judgement.

14:14-20 uses the metaphor of harvest. There is a vivid picture of the harvest of the unrighteous (**14:17-20**). The harvest of the righteous, spelt out so clearly in Matthew's Gospel is passed over very quickly in **14:16**.

Revelation 15 raises the curtain on the seven angels, bowls and last plagues. But first, there is rejoicing in heaven. Anticipating judgement, John sees a 'great and marvellous sign' (**15:1**). His vision includes a victory song of Moses, making connections with Israel's victory song after the Exodus (**Exodus 15**) and Moses' final song before he died (**Deuteronomy 32**).

Revelation 16 itemizes seven bowls and plagues. To some extent these plagues (sores, blood, blood, heat, darkness, frogs, earthquake) parallel the plagues in Egypt before the Exodus (blood, frogs, gnats, flies, livestock, boils, hail, locusts, darkness, firstborn).

➤ STARTING IT

True plagues
✪ ✪

List on postcards the ten plagues of Egypt from **Exodus 7-11**. Now add ten more of your own. We suggest grass, oranges, weevils, snow, laughter, bricks, earwax, second-born, distractions and sick. Ask members to sort them into two bins labelled 'bucket of death' and 'barrel of laughs'. Introduce the session and the connection between this passage and Exodus.

Don't go there
✪

If you meet in a hall or large room play this game. Use masking tape to mark out an area about two metres square. The idea is not to go into this area. Choose someone to be 'on'. They must try and pull others into the square, at which point they are also 'on'. The only resistance allowed is passive. Members can cling on to each other.

Make the point that the square represents the 'tabernacle of the Testimony' (**15:5**). Nobody can go in there until God's judgement is completed (**15:8**). This session is going to be about God's judgement.

Raiders of the lost ark
✪ ✪

The theme of death and judgement is spelled out very dramatically in the scene towards the end of the first Indiana Jones film, *Raiders of the Lost Ark*. When the ark is opened, everyone who watches is destroyed. It would be a good clip with which to begin the session.

Avenging angels
✪

A good opening track would be 'Calling All Avenging Angels' by Space.

Persecution
✪ ✪ ✪

Read an account of a persecuted Christian or group of Christians. (You may have decided to do this already.) The Keston Institute (formerly Keston

PAGE 44

SESSION 7

College) or Amnesty International would be good sources of up-to-date stories (addresses on page 28).

➤ TEACHING IT

Background painting
✪ ✪ ✪

Select prints and posters of well-known paintings so that you can point out that often the background is painted with remarkable care.

Now hand out slips of paper with the following verses written on them and ask volunteers to read them out. After each verse, briefly explain how it contributes to the background of this passage.

Luke 10:2
Jesus saw his disciples' work as 'harvesting'. Evangelism is reaping the harvest of those whose readiness to turn to God is like being 'ripe'.

Revelation 14:15-16
And John's vision shows it happening.

Exodus 29:42-43
From the time of Moses, God meets his people in the tabernacle and, later, in the temple.

Revelation 15:5-6a
But in this passage when the temple is opened there are terrible consequences.

Psalm 79:12
The Psalmist hoped God would judge and punish his people's enemies.

Leviticus 26:18
But the same sevenfold punishment had been threatened on Israel if disobedient.

Revelation 16:1
And this vision previews it happening to the whole earth.

Trumpets or plagues?
✪ ✪ ✪

Use this old game. Give everyone a bit of paper and ask them to make a small doodle on it. Then pass the paper to somebody else who has to make the doodle into a recognizable picture. Prize for the best if you want.

Make the point that the doodles were incomplete pictures but have now been completed.

You could also prepare some pictures that are only partially completed. If you want to be thoroughly biblical then prepare exactly one third of each picture and ask members to complete the other two thirds.

PAGE 45

SESSION 7

Now refer to session 5 where the trumpets sounded their notes of judgement. The trumpets heralded partial destruction, but now, with the bowls and plagues, judgement on those who remain outside Christ is full and final.

Explain again that Revelation is not designed to be chronological. These visions represent God's verdict on human sinfulness and the inevitability of final judgement. Revelation is a pictorial representation of teaching covered clearly elsewhere in the Bible. Read **1 Thessalonians 4:13-18** slowly and quietly, even if you have used it in other sessions. Be sure members have understood the Bible's clear teaching about Jesus' second coming before they grapple with the nuances of this extended metaphor in Revelation.

Mercy or what?

This passage focuses very clearly on God's wrath. Take time to discuss whether members feel more aware of God's mercy or his wrath. Conclude with prayers of gratitude for our salvation through the work of Christ. Pray for those we are in touch with who don't yet know that salvation.

Thieftime

Draw lots to determine who is to be the thief. Everyone needs to put a Post-it note on their back. Turn on some loud music and mingle. The aim is for the thief, who remains anonymous, to steal Post-it notes without being noticed. Play several times and have a prize for the best thief.

Read **Revelation 16:15**. Make the link with **Matthew 24:43-44**.

Make the point that being prepared for theft makes you more alert. Those who await Jesus' return and judgement need to be constantly alert. Otherwise it is like being caught naked in public.

➤ DOING IT

Caught out

Tell members that the next part is completely confidential. Ask them to write on the Work-out sheet brief headings of things they do, but would not like to be caught doing at the final judgement. Pray a general prayer of confession/ forgiveness. It would be good to make this feel more formal by reading the absolution from *The Alternative Service Book* or *The Book of Common Prayer*. Then do the next activity.

Thank you very much

Invite members to use the bottom half of the Work-out sheet to list things for which they are grateful to God.

When they have finished, invite them to tear the sheet in half, to keep the list of things they are grateful for, but to destroy the list of sins. You could make a point of having a dramatic destruction of the 'sin papers', perhaps using fire, vats of concentrated acid, a shredder, a labrador or something more imaginative. Of course we disclaim all liability for accidents so caused.

WORK-OUT

I am aware of the following things I would not like to be caught doing:

....

....

....

....

....

....

....

....

I am grateful to God because...

....

....

....

....

....

....

....

....

SESSION 8: REVELATION 17:1 - 19:10

Who's Mighty Now?

◆ TEACHING POINT
The glamour of sin disguises its folly and doomed nature.

◆ GROUP AIM
For members to delight in goodness and keep clear of sin.

EQUIPMENT CHECKLIST

(Depending on which sections you tackle, you may need)
- Bibles
- Pens and paper
- Balloons
- Plastic sheet and washing-up liquid
- Coconut shy equipment
- Work-out sheets
- Smelly things

LEADERS' GUIDE

The seven bowls are emptied, but now we have a long section which shows us the working out of bowl number seven – God's wrath coming with great force against 'Babylon the Great'. This passage is a good illustration of the fact that Revelation is not a series of events set down in chronological order. We've already heard twice about the fall of Babylon (**14:8**; **16:19**) and now we hear and see it in more detail.

Chapter 16 ended with people verbally cursing God. Chapter 17 shows us the living embodiment of blasphemy. This is the outward appearance, all success and glamour. Chapter 18 shows the spiritual reality of the futility of fighting against God, including (**18:9** onwards) the reaction to it of the ungodly. We are shown the godly reaction, too. This gets us pretty much to the end of the 'bad news' side of Revelation. If people are feeling a bit 'punch-drunk' after several sessions of 'judgement' passages, remind them of the 'good news' bits that have been interspersed, and reassure them that we're about to enter the glorious finishing straight. But there's a serious challenge to us first.

BIBLE BACKGROUND

Images of adultery and prostitution, standing for unfaithfulness to God, abound throughout the Bible. We can trace a trail from the warning of **Exodus 34:15-16**, through **Judges 2:16-17** and many of the prophets, to **Matthew 16:4** and **James 4:4**, and we will barely have scratched the surface. Unfaithfulness to his rule is a big issue for God. This is the culmination of such images, and the scandalous woman in chapter 17 is the absolute opposite of the woman we met in chapter 12, who stood for the faithful community of the people of God. For the many waters on which she sits, remember the comment on the sea in the Bible Background to session 6.

The description of the beast – it 'once was, now is not, and will' come back

SESSION 8

(**17:8**) – may well be a reference to the persecuting Emperor Nero. A myth grew up that some time after his death he would reappear and wreak further havoc. More directly, the description is clearly a perversion of God's own attributes – he who was, and is, and is to come. The beast symbolizes powers which oppose God and try to usurp his rule.

17:9 and its following verses and **17:18** clearly refer to Rome, built on seven hills and the great power that oppressed Christians when the revelation was given. Attempts to identify the beast and the city with particular modern-day political figures or powers tend to be hysterical and are unnecessary. Iraq has been a favourite candidate for this role in the 1990s, but Rome has its counterparts in most ages and they do not necessarily equate with the chosen political bugbear of western democracy. Another aspect of the 'seven hills' description is that hills symbolized power, which together with the 'perfect' number seven gives an idea of the (temporary) dominance of the beast.

➤ STARTING IT

Slippery slope ✪

Give pairs of group members a different topic each and ask them to chart the possible stages in a transition from one extreme to another: married faithfulness to adultery; honesty to theft; love to murder, and so on. If they enjoy role-play you could set this up as a courtroom scene, with counsels offering a defence of the progression from stage to stage. Make the point that it's easy to take little steps along a path of wrong-doing, convincing ourselves that it's all right really, until we can't turn back.

Slippery sheet ✪

This is another way to make the same point. If you can run this activity outside, get a plastic sheet and a supply of water and have a slide. Remove any jewellery first. Once you get going, you can't stop, especially if you add a bit of washing-up liquid to the water.

Blasphem-eh? ✪ ✪

If your group isn't familiar with the term 'blasphemy', look together at **Exodus 20:7** and discuss what it means in practice. Need it be restricted to the use of words? Add **Revelation 16:21** for an additional slant.

➤ TEACHING IT

Balloon burst ✪ ✪

Brainstorm the names of people in the news who have been puffed up with fame or success and have then crashed. Draw their faces, with whatever skill your group can muster, on balloons and then pop them, having briefly discussed the reasons why they have lost their way. It wouldn't be a bad idea to pray for some of them, if their troubles are recent.

SESSION 8

Foxy lady
✪ ✪ ✪

Read **17:1-6**. Get the group to pick out the glamorous aspects of the picture presented: what might entice people to follow this woman? Summarize **17:7-18** to give an idea of the glamour and power portrayed, and make the point that although this is a world power, not an individual, the same principles hold true on an individual level. If you have time, read **Proverbs 7:6-23** together to reinforce the point.

Coconut shy
✪ ✪ ✪

Have fun knocking things down – real coconuts, skittles, balloons, Ming vases or whatever. Foam balls are probably the safest things to throw, but tailor the activity to your group. Then (perhaps turning on lots of extra lights to go with **18:1**) read **18:1-8** and pick out the reasons for 'Babylon's' downfall. These include pride, trusting in wealth, leading others astray – and more. After this, point out that Babylon's fate illustrates the loneliness and brutalized nature of those who give themselves up to sin (compare the apparent partnership of **17:3** with **17:16**).

Nightmare TV
✪

Divide the group into three TV crews, and give them a few minutes to prepare reports based on **18:9-10**, **11-17a** or **17b-20**. Each report should contain a bit of 'editorial' on why the disaster has happened. Have the reports acted out. One member should take the role of a 'summarizer in the studio', commenting on the finality of **18:21-24**.

Hallelujah!
✪ ✪

Find out what are the highest terms of praise and approval in vogue with your group members at the moment. The days of 'cowabunga!', 'bostin'!' and 'fab!' are gone, so what has replaced them? Then make sure the group know that 'Hallelujah!' means 'Praise the Lord!' It's a term that never goes out of fashion, because God is always worthy to be praised. If your group members like singing, this would be a good place to have a praise song.

Great culminations
✪ ✪ ✪

Ask people to talk about when they had to wait a long time for something good to happen – to get someone to go out with them, to get a present or CD, or whatever. Read **19:6-7** again, making sure that people understand that the Lamb is Jesus and the bride is his people. The Bible we've used to prepare this resource has 1370 pages; the 'wedding of the Lamb' comes on page 1367. Get the group to check its page number in their own Bibles. That's an awfully long wait for the most fantastic moment in history. What a wonderful feeling that's going to be!

Lamb-centred
✪ ✪

Read **19:9-10**. Explain that the end of **19:10** means essentially that the message about Jesus is the message of God. The Jews often referred to God's Spirit as the Spirit of prophecy, and that is identified here with the gospel, the good news about Jesus. As the angel points out, the only fitting response to that is to worship God. With that thought in mind, give the group time to complete the Work-out sheet, expressing their response to God's invitation to be one of the guests at the wedding. These responses should be honest and so kept private, but try to make an opportunity later for anyone who wants to discuss their response with you.

SESSION 8

Drum it up ✪ ✪

Let the group make a lot of noise. Start very quietly, perhaps with fingers drumming very softly on a table, and build a crescendo using whatever is lying around the room. BUT be sure to finish by moving from the drumming to a group shout of the words in **19:6b-8**. Try to make the shout as loud as the drumming. Have a couple of practice runs to work out the best version, and then really go for it.

➤ DOING IT

Pollution ✪

In the group, draw up a league table for the worst smells ever. Produce some bad smells by whatever means you like to create an appropriate atmosphere (old fish is a good one). Do the same for the worst substances ever. (Make a league table – *don't* bring them in.)

So... ✪

Look together at **1 Kings 11:1-6** and then **2 Timothy 4:10**. What's the message for us? Brainstorm about what things threaten to draw us away from love of God and obedience to him, then read the warning in **18:4**.

Memory verse ✪ ✪ ✪

Revelation 18:4
Then I heard another voice from heaven say: 'Come out of her, my people, so that you will not share in her sins, so that you will not receive any of her plagues....'

Pray ✪ ✪ ✪

Pray.

WORK-OUT

Then the angel said to me, 'Write: "Blessed are those who are invited to the wedding supper of the Lamb!"'

(Revelation 19:9)

**JESUS, THE LAMB OF GOD,
the First and the Last,
who is alive for ever and ever,**

INVITES YOU TO HIS WEDDING SUPPER.

Dress is your choice; no need to bring a bottle;
just bring your faith.

R S V P

MY RESPONSE:

I will/will not be coming to the wedding feast.

My reason is ....

If I'm coming, I'm most looking forward to...

If I'm not coming, the thing I'd rather be doing than attending the high point of all history is .... I must be mad.

SESSION 9: REVELATION 19:11 - 22:5

Winners and Losers

◆ TEACHING POINT
For those who endure, heaven will be great, and worth waiting for.

◆ GROUP AIM
For members to be eager for the end of the world!

EQUIPMENT CHECKLIST

(Depending on which sections you tackle, you may need)
- Bibles
- Pens and paper
- Golf equipment and obstacles
- Work-out sheets
- Watch or clock with second hand
- Arty-crafty stuff
- Horrible things
- Chocolates
- Slips of paper for banquet

LEADERS' GUIDE

This is an exciting section of Revelation – as if any of it has not been! It's not unknown for people to get a bit hysterical about the events outlined in chapters 19 and 20, so make sure that your group focuses on what we're actually told, and remember the context of the rest of Revelation and the rest of the Bible. That's the best cure for hysteria.

If you can manage it, have only one light on for this session and, at an appropriate time, draw attention to it in the context of **21:23** and **22:5**.

BIBLE BACKGROUND

As with the last session, we can see here that chronology is not a concern of John in setting down his vision. He seems to be referring to the same event in **16:12-16, 17:7-14, 19:11-21** and **20:1-10** – one great uprising against God which will be put to an end by Jesus' return. That raises the question of what and when the 'thousand years' will be, especially given the fact that the Bible seems to think in terms of Jesus coming back once and once only, not in a series of comeback performances like Frank Bruno or Status Quo.

The three main theories about the thousand years (the 'millennium') can all be argued quite reasonably. **Pre-millennialists** contend that Jesus will return to lead a 'heavenly' kingdom on earth, interrupted by Satan's rebellion before God's final intervention; the judgement of all the dead follows. **Post-millennialists** believe this kingdom will be initiated and run by the Church, with Jesus not returning until Satan's final fling. **Amillenniallists** hold that the thousand years (which, in the context of Revelation, are unlikely to be literal) are happening now, with Jesus' people ruling with him in a spiritual sense; Satan is restricted in what he can do but is allowed in due course to fight with his full, doomed power until Jesus intervenes to establish God's kingdom and end all rebellion.

SESSION 9

We do not take a view here about which of these three positions is most persuasive; that's for you to decide in the light of the teaching of the whole Bible on these matters. It's one of the areas where, under the Lordship of Christ, Christians can disagree without feeling they have to fight their corner.

The description of the new heaven and earth are full of echoes from the first two chapters of Genesis. It would be well worth reading those chapters before teaching this; if you have time it would be useful to let the group compare the two passages. In Revelation we see the consummation of what God has intended for his people from the very beginning.

There's a similar 'finishing off' feel to the detailed description of the holy city. As well as being a cube (the 'perfect' shape), it recalls previous aspects of Israel's religious history. The inner sanctuary of the original temple was a cube, and the high priest's breastplate held precious stones with names inscribed on them. The picture John gives us of the holy city is the culmination of the signs of God's presence with his people throughout biblical history.

Note that there is *one* throne (**22:1**) belonging to God and the Lamb. Together, these two make up the city's *one* temple and *one* light (**21:22-23**). A clearer indication of the identification of Father and Son in the Godhead would be harder to find – unless it's Jesus' applying to himself the precise title of Alpha and Omega (**22:13**) ascribed to 'the Lord God' (**1:8**).

➤ STARTING IT

Manifesto
✪ ✪

Brainstorm (with as little sour disillusionment as possible) on the sort of things that governments and political parties promise in their manifestos. Do people know of any specific examples in recent times? Perhaps you should do a session sometime on 'the Christian and politics'? In **21:3-5** God is speaking of himself and making huge promises about what he will do. Discuss what difference these promises would make if they were in operation in people's lives now. Their fulfilment is in the future, but God swears that he can be trusted. Share reasons why we can take him at his word.

Crazy putt
✪

Set up a couple of holes of 'crazy golf' and give everyone a chance to have a go at some of the course. Which hole did people find most frustrating? We all get a bit uptight when we can't reach our goals easily. Make the point that in this session we reach all sorts of fulfilment: the culmination of the vision; the end of the book; an understanding of our destination as individual Christians; reassurance about God's eternal, loving rule.

SESSION 9

Heavenly thoughts ✪

Ask everyone to write a single sentence expressing their idea of what heaven will contain. Read them all out and ask people to guess who has written what. The final two chapters of Revelation give a great feel for what heaven is going to be like – though it would be inconsistent of us to take all the details as being literally true, after what we've said about the rest of the book.

➤ STARTING IT

What happened first? ✪ ✪

Distribute the 'You've just...' slips from the Work-out sheet and ask group members to guess what has just happened as each is acted out. Make the point that what happens always affects what we see next. Before the new heaven and earth come in their fullness, evil needs its final defeat.

Who's boss? ✪ ✪ ✪

Read aloud from **Revelation 19:11 - 20:14**. Pause after each paragraph for people to suggest answers to the questions 'Who wins this bit?' and 'What's the effect of that?' Hint: God wins the lot, and evil is thoroughly trounced. You knew that.

Who's Jesus? ✪ ✪

Starting with **19:11-16** and moving on to other parts of the Bible, brainstorm all the titles and descriptions of Jesus the group can think of. When the supply starts to dry up, take time for worship, praise or silence. He is so wonderful!

Which banquet? ✪ ✪ ✪

Draw lots to divide the group into two. Give one half chocolates and the other a slip of paper saying, 'You're on the menu!' Draw attention to the two banquets we have in this chapter, in **19:9** (last session) and **19:17-18**. At one, people will presumably get the most wonderful food. At the other, they *are* the food. The great thing is, we don't get to one or the other by drawing lots: it's a question of our response to the wonderful Lord Jesus.

What-millennialist? ✪ ✪

Run through the different positions, summarized in the Bible background, which Christians take regarding the 'thousand years' of **20:2,7**. Encourage members to think that question through for themselves, but stress that other parts of the Bible have something to say on the question, and that our conclusion is not something which is central to our salvation.

Trust time ✪ ✪ ✪

Invite a few members to choose which of the others they would trust to be able to judge accurately an interval of thirty seconds. Then get the people they've picked to shut their eyes (blindfold them if *you* don't trust them) and ask them to put their hands up when they judge thirty seconds have passed after you give the start signal. Give a prize to the winning combination. Point out that we can all expect attacks of evil in the future. Ask group members how willing they are to trust Jesus' sense of timing, and so to endure the tough times that may come.

It makes me mad ✪ ✪

Brainstorm the things that make group members angry or sad. Read **21:1-8** and help them see that both the cause and effect of their anger and sadness will be swept away at the time of God's choosing.

SESSION 9

Cityscape
★

Read **21:9-27** and then have an arty-crafty session, painting or making a version of the heavenly city, as beautiful as people can make it. Try to have lots of glitter and brightly coloured stuff available as well as more basic things. You may be able to get some cheap costume jewellery to stick on. When the city is as finished as time and creativity allow, bring out some horrible things (use your discretion) and ask how people would feel if you were to add these to their beautiful work. Suggest that this links with God's feelings about our world now and what he longs for and intends to give us. Allow a few moments for people to think or pray about that.

➤ DOING IT

Dream home
★ ★ ★

Ask people to think for a few moments and then describe their dream home – location, contents, gadgets and so on. Read **22:1-5** and make the point that the heavenly city will be better than any they can possibly dream of. Discuss the way in which people usually use the phrase 'the end of the world' (as in: 'It's not...') For Christians the 'end of the world' is a good thing, because it will bring heaven in.

Worship
★ ★ ★

Have a time of worship focusing on the idea of heaven, using songs which take it as a motivation for praise, readings which explore its wonder, the model city you made or painted earlier, and anything else which helps your group respond to God for the amazing destination he has lined up for you.

Memory verse
★ ★ ★

Revelation 21:3
And I heard a loud voice from the throne saying, 'Now the dwelling of God is with men, and he will live with them. They will be his people, and God himself will be with them and be their God.'

WORK-OUT

You have 15 seconds in which to act as if you've just found a cactus in your underpants.

You have 15 seconds in which to act as if you've just been tickled.

You have 15 seconds in which to act as if you've just stepped onto the dance-floor.

You have 15 seconds in which to act as if you've just climbed a tree to escape from a rhino.

You have 15 seconds in which to act as if you've just opened a maths GCSE paper.

You have 15 seconds in which to act as if you've just picked up a baby.

SESSION 10: REVELATION 22:6 - 21

Ending Up!

◆ TEACHING POINT
A reminder to live expecting Jesus to come again suddenly.

◆ GROUP AIM
For the group to go through a summary of the main themes of Revelation.

EQUIPMENT CHECKLIST

(Depending on which sections you tackle, you may need)
- Bibles
- Prepared visual aid of Jesus' titles
- Copy of Work-out sheet
- Dictionary
- Dirty and clean clothes
- Copy of *The Book of Heroic Failures* by Stephen Pile (Routledge & Kegan Paul, 1979)
- Flipchart or OHP and screen
- Biscuits, coins, two T-shirts (one clean, one dirty) and bread rolls (one fresh, one very stale)

LEADERS' GUIDE

Conveniently, we are going to find this passage offers a nice summary of where we have been in the whole book. This means that you may want to use some 'memory joggers' by repeating some of the activities from your study of Revelation that have gone really well. Remember to make the point of the activity again rather than just using great games for their own sake.

BIBLE BACKGROUND

There are four key sections in this passage:

God's word (**22:6-10**). God speaks to people through his word. The whole of the book of Revelation is designed to make things clear, 'to show his servants what must soon take place' (**1:1**). Angels, prophets and servants have all played their part (**22:6**), but with the completion of Revelation God has revealed *all* he is going to reveal. His word is complete.

God's work (**22:11-15**). What is the work of God? It has been creation and redemption. We now await the culmination of those two acts – final judgement. **22:11** looks a little unclear at first. It is not encouraging wrongdoers to stick with their evil ways, but rather is stating that there will be a time when people have fixed their destiny. This section has three mighty metaphors of the destiny of the saved:

1. Clean robes   2. Access to the tree of life   3. Entry into God's city.

God's blessing (**22:16-17**). The shortest summary of the gospel is 'Come'. All you need to do is to want to be blessed by God. Through Jesus, both the ancestor and descendant of David (clever that), this blessing is available. These two

SESSION 10

verses summarize the last section of Revelation, which summarizes the whole book, which summarizes the whole Bible. These verses see Jesus speaking in his own name, in the first person, rather than hearing testimony about him.

God's curse (**22:18-19**). God's curse is not on those who differ slightly with you over the interpretation of a verse of Revelation. Remember this chapter is a summary and thus the curse is for any who, according to Michael Wilcock, 'alter the gospel to suit themselves' (*The Message of Revelation,* IVP).

Finally we have an epilogue (**22:20-21**). There is a reminder, if ever it was needed after our studies, that this book has been about grace for all God's people until the moment when Jesus returns. We must continue to live as if that day will be soon.

➤ STARTING IT

Who said that? Read 22:6-21 but ask members to observe who is speaking at each point. Look out for the angel, John, Jesus, Spirit (and God's people, the bride).

Sooner or later Write these sentences on a flipchart or OHP acetate:

It will be my birthday soon.
I hope the bus comes soon.
Soon and very soon, we're going to see the Lord.
West Bromwich Albion will get promotion soon.

Discuss, briefly, how long 'soon' means in each one. Make the point that the length of time covered by the word 'soon' depends entirely on context. Read **Revelation 22:6-21**, preferably from the New International Version where the word 'soon' appears four times. Ask members to listen out for each use. Remind them that 'soon' in Revelation can either mean 'after a short period of time' or 'suddenly'.

Titles Remind members of how Jesus-centred this book has been by making a visual aid that displays all the titles of Jesus, from this passage alone:

Alpha and Omega (**22:13**)   First and Last (**22:13**)
Beginning and End (**22:13**)   Root and Offspring of David (**22:16**)
Bright Morning Star (**22:16**)   Lord (**22:20**)

You could use the first part of the Work-out sheet for this.

Then spend some time looking back through the whole book for other titles and add them to the visual aid, together with references.

Famous last words Many famous last words have been the cause of much mirth. The general who looked across at the enemy troops and said, 'Don't worry, they couldn't

SESSION 10

hit an elephant at this dist...' is perhaps the most quoted. There is also a famous tombstone which, allegedly, bears the epitaph, 'I told you I was ill.' Spend a few moments chatting about instances such as these. If you can get hold of a copy of Stephen Pile's *The Book of Heroic Failures* you may well be able to entertain your group for, ooh, several minutes.

➤ TEACHING IT

Why come to Jesus?
✪ ✪

22:6-16 make a good basis for a five-point evangelistic talk, identified by Murray Robertson in his study book *The Future of Humanity* (Bible Reading Fellowship, 1993).

We should come to Jesus:

1. because the message is true (**22:6**)
2. because he is coming back again (**22:7**)
3. because nobody else, not even the angel, bringer of the message of Revelation, is worthy of worship (**22:8-9**)
4. because he will judge (**22:12**)
5. because he alone cleanses (**22:14**).

Complete word
✪ ✪ ✪

Use a flipchart or OHP for this. Start a word by writing any letter on the chart. Then hand the pen to the next person who adds another letter, again having in mind a complete word. After each pass of the pen the new player can either add a letter or challenge the previous writer to complete the word. Give a point for a successful challenge or for completing a word once challenged. Have a dictionary handy.

Example 1
Player 1 writes m (thinking *man*)
Player 2 writes a (thinking *machine*)
Player 3 writes t (thinking *material*)
Player 4 writes c (thinking *matches*)
Player 5 writes h (thinking *matching*)
Player 6 writes m (thinking *matchmaker*)
Player 7 is stumped so challenges
Player 6 writes *matchmaker* and wins a point.

Example 2
Player 1 writes b (thinking *bag*)
Player 2 writes e (thinking *best*)
Player 3 writes a (thinking *beauty*)
Player 4 writes s (thinking *beast*)
Player 5 writes t (thinking *beastly*)
Player 6 writes l (thinking *beastly*)
Player 7 writes i (thinking *beastliness*)
Player 8 writes e (not thinking)
Player 9 challenges
Player 8 concedes; point to player 9

Of course, if you have a small group you just go back to player 1 when you run out of participants. After a few rounds, make the point from the Bible base on **Revelation 22:6-10** that God's word is complete.

Dirty work
✪ ✪ ✪

Describe some job or other of a practical nature that involves getting messy. Go into glorious detail. Then talk about the cleaning power of soap and water and how nice it is to wash and change afterwards. Demonstrate if you

SESSION 10

want with a set of muddy overalls which you exchange for a clean pair. Explain that this is a picture of Jesus' work. We are washed and have access to the holy city and the tree of life. Read **Revelation 21:2**, **Genesis 2:9,17** and then **Revelation 22:14** as reminders.

Blessings and curses
✪ ✪ ✪

Set up a series of stark choices. For instance:

A pristine wrapped chocolate biscuit; a horribly melted one
A £1 coin; a plastic coin
A clean white T-shirt; a dirty white T-shirt
A fresh bread roll; a mouldy bread roll.

Give members (draw lots to find out who) the free choice to keep one item from each of the contrasting pairs. Read **22:16-19** and remind members that the choice between life and death is set out very starkly. Challenge them to stick to their decisions and to keep working on their friends.

➤ DOING IT

Graceland
✪ ✪ ✪

Tell the story of Elvis Presley. Remind people that his home 'Graceland' in Memphis, Tennessee, was filled with all the things he liked as a child. He lived on cheeseburgers (which contributed to his early death). Go into any further details you know. Maybe play the song 'Graceland' by Paul Simon as background.

Explain that heaven on earth is impossible. We may make money and be able to live in luxury, but the greatest luxury we can have today is to live under the grace of God, by which we are saved. This is why John ends his book with a message of grace to all God's people.

Pray that the lessons learnt in Revelation will make an impact. Pray for each other and end with the words of the grace.

Remember it?
✪ ✪

On the second half of the Work-out sheet are various words that have been key to understanding Revelation. Go through them and check they have been understood. Let members write brief notes next to them to take home.

Memory verses
✪ ✪

Want a change from learning verses from Revelation? **Ephesians 1:9-10** accurately summarizes this section of the book.

'And he made known to us the mystery of his will according to his good pleasure, which he purposed in Christ, to be put into effect when the times will have reached their fulfilment – to bring all things in heaven and on earth together under one head, even Christ.'

Alternatively use **Revelation 22:20**. 'He who testifies to these things says, "Yes, I am coming soon." Amen. Come, Lord Jesus.'

WORK-OUT

TITLES

- The three titles of Jesus from 22:13 are:

    1................................ 2................................ 3................................

- The two titles of Jesus from 22:16 are:

    1................................ 2................................

- The title of Jesus from 22:20 is:

    ....

- Other titles of Jesus in the Bible:..

    ....

REMEMBER IT?

Apocalypse..

Letters..

Throne..

Judgement..

Trumpets..

Environment..

Babylon..

Beast..

Heaven..

Jesus..

About CYFA

CYFA (14-18 year-olds) and **Pathfinders** (11-14s) are organizations which, as part of the Church Pastoral Aid Society, support the youth work of local churches throughout the UK and Ireland.

Help is offered to local leaders through training (including annual events for full-time and voluntary leaders), members' events, Bible teaching resources, Ventures (great holidays with Christian teaching) and regular mailings for member groups.

Membership is easy, costs only £50 a year (for the whole church) at the time of going to press and entitles leaders to all the above benefits plus discounts on the training events.

CPAS is an evangelical, home missionary society which exists to strengthen Anglican churches to evangelize, teach and pastor people of all ages.

For under-11s **CPAS** has **Explorers, Climbers and Scramblers**.

CHURCH PASTORAL AID SOCIETY
Athena Drive, Tachbrook Park, WARWICK CV34 6NG

Tel: (01926) 334242
Fax: (01926) 337613

Email: ycd@cpas.org.uk
Internet: http://www.cpas.org.uk

Other Resources from CPAS

Books that should be indispensable in a youth leader's library are:

CPAS Code		
03428	Young People and the Bible	Phil Moon (Marshalls, 1993)
03591	Christian Youth Work	Phil Moon and Mark Ashton (Monarch, 1995)

Other books in the same series as *The End is in Sight*

C16127	All Together Forever	Ephesians
C16129	Pressure Points	Issues that concern teenagers
C16130	Harping On?	Six Psalms
C16132	Repeat Prescription	The Ten Commandments
C16131	You'd Better Believe It!	Christian doctrine
C16134	Powered Up	Key moments from Acts
C16135	Just About Coping	Issues that teenagers have to cope with
C16136	Mission in Action	Broadening your group's horizons
C16137	People with a Purpose	Ten Old Testament characters
C16139	Outlawed by Grace	Galatians
C16138	Didn't He Used To Be Dead?	Jesus
C16142	You'd Better Believe This Too!	More Christian doctrine
C16141	Another Brick in the Wall	Nehemiah

Books from CPAS to resource your meetings:

C16128	Know Ideas!	Ideas to put into your programme
C16140	Know Ideas! 2	And some more...
C16143	Know Ideas! 3	Guess
C16133	Rave On	Ideas and principles for worship
C18006	The ART of 14-18s	Age-range tools for leading groups

CHURCH PASTORAL AID SOCIETY

Athena Drive, Tachbrook Park, WARWICK CV34 6NG

Tel: (01926) 334242   24-hour Sales Ansaphone: (01926) 335855